Mentored to Perfection

Mentored to Perfection

The Masculine Terms of Success in Academia

By Simone Dennis and Alison Behie

LEXINGTON BOOKS

Lanham • Boulder • New York • London

Published by Lexington Books
An imprint of The Rowman & Littlefield Publishing Group, Inc.
4501 Forbes Boulevard, Suite 200, Lanham, Maryland 20706
www.rowman.com

6 Tinworth Street, London SE11 5AL, United Kingdom

British Library Cataloguing in Publication Information Available

Library of Congress Cataloging-in-Publication Data Available

ISBN 978-1-66691-477-1 (cloth)
ISBN 978-1-66691-478-8 (electronic)
ISBN 978-1-66691-479-5 (pbk.)

*We dedicate this work to our informants, without
whom there would be no book.*

Contents

Acknowledgments

Simone wishes to acknowledge the kindness of her friend Deane Fergie, who gave very insightful feedback on early and embarrassingly rough drafts. This work is so much the richer for her involvement.

Simone also wishes to thank sincerely her dear friend, Andrew Dawson, who regularly checked in on the progress of the work, and on Simone herself, and offered sage advice when either was ailing.

Simone thanks Max, Keaka, Wren, and Tina for their support.

Alison wishes to thank all of the women who have served as mentors for her either formally or informally over the years. Aside from Alison's mother, the most prominent of these women is Mary SM Pavelka, who has been her supervisor, colleague, and friend over the past 20 years. Alison would not be the researcher, academic, or mother she is without Mary's advice and guidance.

Alison also wants to thank the little people for whom she does most everything—her children: Georgia, Riley, and Cordelia. She hopes that her imperfectness shows her children that life can be messy, chaotic, and absolutely wonderful all at the same time. While Alison thanks all of her family members for their support, she especially wants to recognize James for his unwavering belief in her. Alison could not do half of what she does without his acting as sounding board and cheerleader.

Simone and Alison want to thank their colleague and friend Professor Kylie Message for her feedback on this work, even when she was far too busy to even consider doing such a thing.

We dedicate this work to our informants, without whom there would be no book.

We also acknowledge the efforts of our own university to make things better and more inclusive for women; that effort is amply demonstrated by the fact that robust critique, such as the kind we make in this book of not just this but all institutions, is welcomed and taken seriously. There could hardly be a better start to institutional change than institutional willingness to entertain it.

Introduction

QUESTIONING LAUDABLE THINGS IS HARD

In this book, we explore mentoring. As we explain in this introduction, we do not restrict ourselves to an analysis of named mentoring programs. Our offering encompasses many less obvious manifestations of the practice. Our analysis demonstrates how mentoring (ironically) undergirds and replicates the patriarchal structures it seeks to trouble. We do not offer a comprehensive look at the neoliberal university in which mentoring is presently valuable; the interested reader should consult Lipton's (2020) excellent and insightful text for a comprehensive ethnographically inspired entrée. In this book we stay with mentoring—but not only the named versions of the practice.

This has been a hard book for us to write, because the women involved in mentoring programs did not see their practice in the ways that we have seen it in our analysis. In fact, it would be fair to say that none of our interlocutors would consider participating in mentoring relations if they thought they were involved in undergirding patriarchal structures. Indeed, for a great many of them, getting involved in mentoring was getting directly involved in confronting patriarchal practices and presumptions; for them, this was good and very important work to do.

The kind of material we got from our informants about being involved in mentoring is markedly different from some of the work we have seen elsewhere, such as that remarked upon by equity and social justice commentators like Ferrara (2020). Ferrara recently observed in *Academic Matters* magazine that university policy is often unfriendly to women, even when it is created by women, because "some female policy makers are senior academics who have managed to climb the ladder by emulating the lifestyle and productivity of their male counterparts" (2020: np). Perhaps because of her status as commentator, Ferrara has found herself serving as a disclosure point, noting that she has heard some distressing "confessions." For some women who have confided in her, the (value accorded) male institutional dominance was so obvious that they felt it would be better if they adopted male ways of being rather than continuing to struggle as females. In scholarly literature, this "becoming male" takes two main forms.

The first involves engaging in evident dominance over other women. We really did not see much of this in our own investigation. On the whole, neither senior nor junior women felt as though they were entangled in something akin to gendered violence, in which senior academic women internalize masculinist practices of aggression directed at their juniors There are, though, examples aplenty in literature. Fitzgerald (2014), Burkinshaw (2015), Blackmore and Sachs (2007), van den Brink and Benschop (2014), and Morley (1999) each detail horribly toxic cultures of female gatekeeping, in which it is revealed that not all women are supportive of other women. As Morley (2013) suggests, the competition between women (for scarce or limited opportunities for funding, publications contracts and promotion) can create sharp rivalries.

The second involves dialling down the female biological (and, as we show in our own offering, socially derived) attributes that might prove disruptive to careers. In one dramatic case reported to Ferrara, a participant decided to have a tubal ligation because she needed to remain competitive with her male counterparts. Another had her eggs harvested and frozen to avoid taking time out for pregnancy and childcare; she believed such preemptive action was necessary for her to continue to compete on equal terms with male colleagues. We collected a few stories of this kind, in which women told us about the difficulties of having children while at the same time trying to be outstanding academics. Although we did not hear about any tubal ligations, we did know, for example, that women in our study were often advised by their mentors on "how to play the baby card" to best effect, and how to ensure the least career disruption when having a child. Our material, then, is less stark than those alarming ones reported to Ferrara.

We think the character of our data is really important to the analysis we run. Even though we certainly do include some stark examples of gender bias in our work, our main claim is that mentoring programs tend to further entail women in exactly the hierarchical relations of patriarchy that are the trouble in the first place, but they're far less noticeable. We are referring here to the ways in which senior women who have mastered the masculine terms of success generously educate junior women in how to replicate those terms. This means that even when mentoring programs look like networking support services for neophytes, they nevertheless replicate the institutional structure they seek to trouble. The generosity that senior women show to junior women as they share their tips and offer their support ironically obscures this ominous outcome, chiefly because it entails participants in debt relations.

Thought of in this way, even in the absence of tubal ligations, our analysis of mentoring is founded on the fact that women's participation in the institution is conditional on them successfully modifying their bodies, their comportments, their language—sometimes reflexively, but very often subtly, and sometimes without even knowing it. Also and equally, it entails a key understanding of women as, at first, departures from an array of male standards (made manifest in everything from grant application processes to the physical built environs of university campuses, which tend to reflect male research accomplishments in their sandstones (or their bricks and mortar, or their verdant wood).[1] It is easy enough to see that, in grant applications for instance, provision is made for deviations from "standard" expectations of (male) research performance. Major granting agencies in Australia allow for maternity and child caring, a kind of accounting that explains and justifies research records that might otherwise be read as inconsistent or lesser compared with a "standard" example. It is certainly sometimes the case that men privilege childcare over research, certainly the case that they take paternity leave under current employment provisions, but not nearly as much as women, who thus remain deviations from the standard. The opportunity to explain the circumstances of deviation from the standard is often institutionally considered a key equalising strategy, but one might suggest that remaining a deviation supports unequal structural relations—even as institutions attempt to liberate women from them. In the context of "benchmark masculinity," where only apparently gender-neutral merit criteria for success are animated with male bias, institutionally endorsed equity programs, like women-only mentoring, are purpose-built to assist women to navigate a prevailing patriarchal milieu (see for example Thornton, 2013). As many analysts have pointed out, under such circumstances, it is difficult for such programs to do anything but offer the best strategies for assimilation into the overarching patriarchal structure, to the extent that the only real path to institutional success is for women to effectively become honorary men (see for example Feteris, 2012; Fitzgerald, 2014; Jenkins, 2014; Ahmed, 2012; Morley, 2011; Puwar, 2004).

Wherever one lands on that question, the question of difference arises— and that's really the thing to which we want to draw attention. Women's difference from the institutional standard is not permitted to rattle, disturb, or change the male standard. Difference is certainly *recognised*, but it is accommodated within an existing paradigm—it is not *paradigm changing*. As we argue herein, the same applies to mentoring relations between senior and junior women. We think this is a crucial thing to recognise because it helps to explain why the efforts, the good will, the resources put into changing things, have had very little demonstrable effect; it all occurs well *within* the paradigm. As we suggest herein, the endurance of institutional patriarchy cannot be satisfactorily explained by theses that issue from within the paradigm—explanations that tend to make much of the lag between institutional investment and its fruition. We think the problem that mentoring tries to solve—the problem of less than equal participation—has to do with the endurance of the recognised, *but never disrupting*, difference of women. Our work disrupts the notion that mentoring is a good solution to the problem of inequitable participation, and we begin it by recognising that when women involve themselves in mentoring programs, they do not think that they are furthering patriarchal forms. Indeed, that's the last thing they think, if our data is anything to go by.

The feeling among our interlocutors that mentoring was supportive of the achievement of institutional gender equity goals is important, first because it alerted us to the value of examining the subtleties of mentoring practice. We detail this value of subtle explorations below. Second, it also allows us to respect the ways in which our informants valued, and gained benefit from, the practices in which they participated. This is because the positivity with which mentoring is regarded is precisely what we have focused on in much of our book. We do not dispute positivity—we look closely at what it might contain in the way of patriarchal replication, and specifically what a lauded generosity might conceal. For the most part, mentoring was understood and experienced as a good thing and, especially, it was understood to be a good and generous thing for a senior woman to do for a junior woman who aspired to be successful in the institution. In general, junior women felt similarly enamoured with mentoring, and with their mentors. In this book, we too argue that mentoring creates honorary men out of women, but, in contrast with other works we analyse, we do not think we can parse that outcome from the "good" bits of mentoring; we instead favour an approach that involves stepping beyond the paradigm altogether.

That entails dealing directly with the joys of mentoring (as opposed to its tubal ligations and its egg-freezing manifestations). Those joys, on our analysis, obscure the structural relations of indebtedness and hierarchy that mentoring in all its forms supports and begets. It is often based in an analysis of generosity, and giving, and the hierarchal relations of debt in which those exchanges entail participants. And, it is set against multiple feminist claims that "the good parts" of mentoring can be parsed from those elements that support patriarchal continuance. In its "good" or as de Vries (2011) terms it, "enabling" form, mentoring can be weaponised against the patriarchy. We explore these now very common feminist ideas, and *we ultimately disagree with them.* Despite our critique, however, it is in the spirit of feminist solidarity that we offer our book.

In that spirit, we have tried to be mindful of the danger of disrespect; our informants have been kind enough to share with us their thoughts and narratives of their experiences. We know that we have produced an analysis that might trouble some of our mentor informants who very sincerely believed in what they were doing, in terms of sharing the benefits of their experience and knowledge of the institution with up and coming women. It might worry our mentee interlocutors, too, many of whom were hoping to see real change in patriarchal structures as a result of building strong female networks in and through their involvement in mentoring practices. As we say in our book, therein lies the power of modern patriarchal forms: they seem to support women, but on closer inspection, they may produce the opposite outcome.

We don't consider ourselves possessed of some especial insight to make these claims—it's more that we have a couple of luxuries. One is of position. As senior women who have achieved institutional success, there's something luxurious about criticising the conditions under which we have both achieved success—we have less to lose than those junior women who might yet attain the status we have both achieved. There is no doubt, though, that our success has cost us in ways we would rather not see those who come after us continue to bear, and so we think our irruption worth the ire it might draw on this score.

Another luxury afforded us is that we're not exactly pioneers. We know we are operating at a point of time when the difficulty of instituting gender equity in the neoliberal university is well known, and during a period when, as is the case for our own institution, there is significant and genuine effort directed to making a better work experience for women. We are unlikely to suffer much for offering up a work that is critical of the techniques used to try to achieve gender equity. We do not want our offering to remain girt by that safety, though; we hope that our work will take the intentions already evident in institutional actions and provoke serious reflexive consideration of how it might be achieved. In this, we share Nigel Rapport's (2003) view, that social structures might not determine the environment and circumstances of individual lives. While Rapport most certainly intended to draw attention to how individuals formulate life projects in the shadow of ostensibly overpowering circumstances, we think institutions, too, might be able to push beyond the structures of their own ideologies. That, we think, is part of deliberately stepping beyond the safety and the comfort of the paradigm that, at least to some extent, has nurtured our own careers. The unsafe and uncomfortable circumstances visited upon institutions by COVID-19 might put institutions in the mood for such introspection in any case; the context in which we offer our work, from our equally luxurious and uncomfortable positions, might very well be timely. We are hopeful that the occurrence of COVID-19 might render stark the idea that we advance in our book: that practices that look like they are working against patriarchal structure and practice can, insidiously, support and undergird them. In the case of mentoring, particular relations and organisations of generous exchanges cloak its inextricable involvement in patriarchal continuance. Perhaps the fact that the emergence of COVID-19 has made clear that women are disadvantaged in the university and other patriarchal systems will lead to a hastening of change; it is difficult to ignore emergent statistics that show how many more women have lost their jobs than have men, for instance. Perhaps the fact that the university cannot be as it was before the virus—for all sorts of reasons—will provide a catalyst for some of the pressing changes that need to be made before we can declare institutional gender equity achieved—or even pursued in a way that might deliver something more than paradigmatic approaches have thus far delivered.

GOOD(?) MENTORING

Mentoring is ubiquitous. Certainly, our workplace, the Australian National University (hereafter ANU), has folded it, in programmatic form, into everyday institutional practice. As we show, mentoring occurs in a multiplicity of other forms that are more difficult to recognise as such. We define *mentoring* as any act or practice in which (within the confines of our project) women are advised on where they stand in relation to their potential success in the institution, and what they can do to achieve that success. This definition puts us in a position to explore how inanimate things, like built environs, become indeed highly animate to effectively communicate to women about their institutional positions—the subject, in fact, of our fourth chapter. In whatever form it occurs, mentoring is now a highly valuable institutional good that serves to connect those who have accomplished success with those who want to achieve it.

As we will demonstrate, the bulk of mentoring literature presumes that mentoring is a kind of social *good* (see for example Gardiner, Tiggemann, Kearns & Marshall, 2007; Diamond, 2010; Mullen & Hutinger, 2008; Meschitti & Lawton-Smith, 2017). Amid this overwhelming positivity there are some (primarily) feminist (e.g., Devos, 2011; de Vries, 2011) and loosely Marxist (e.g., Colley, 2003) scholars who question mentoring's otherwise uncontested goodness. They accuse mentoring programs of recruiting neophytes (particularly women) into the relations of patriarchal production in university contexts. These programs are, as the critique goes, fundamentally involved in drawing women into participation in the conditions of their own domination. Mentoring programs provide a blueprint for the navigation of patriarchal conditions, giving women a way to understand and play a game whose umpires and most dominant players are men. Feminist critics point out that this is a pernicious system not only because one might not be able to accrue any capital of worth in the institutional field if one did not participate, but equally because it delivers results of high value to the institution. Mentoring programs produce increased research outcomes that contribute to the institution's rankings which are, increasingly, tied to its financial fortunes (Devos, 2011).

As we mentioned earlier, some analysts (e.g., de Vries, 2011) suggest that mentoring programs *can* effectively challenge patriarchal institutional cultures and can be pressed into the pursuit and accomplishment of gender equity goals. This is claimed on the basis that mentoring programs also and equally create networks, permit the exchange of ideas, and foster a multiplicity of potentially beneficial relationships between women. The most important thing for readers to know about this book, from its outset, is that we *do not share this view*. In fact, as we also mentioned earlier, this book treats mentoring as a window onto the neoliberal university and its participation in the knowledge economy to argue that mentoring, in *all of its present forms*, replicates its patriarchal hierarchical structures. In our book, we argue that mentoring reveals the hierarchical scaffolding of the institution that members are bidden to ascend. We demonstrate how the terms of participation in mentoring practice, precisely the terms of giving and generosity effectively mask the relations of patriarchal power in which they are deeply entailed. As we say later on, this does not mean that we think mentoring itself should be summarily abandoned. We do think that any form of it that privileges the reproduction of male success should be discontinued. This means rethinking the terms and conditions of success. That is a very big ask; perhaps few want to be pioneers in recrafting it, especially those in whose hands it is currently concentrated. Indeed, most critiques of mentoring leave the conditions of success as they stand intact.

The undergirding feminist critique—that mentoring programs ought not to be about enrolling a novice into a system by which they might be oppressed and really should be about its opposite, appears to be a pretty radical departure from the classical mentoring story (which we explore in detail in our book). Homer's *Odyssey,* usually regarded as the origin story of contemporary mentoring, was expected to produce in the young Telemachus an acquiescent, unrebellious wisdom. The guidance Mentor provided to his young ward was designed to have the effect of keeping the operations of power exactly as they were in Telemachus's father's absence (see Roberts, 1999). Notwithstanding that Telemachus was to inherit his father's kingdom, the fact is that mentoring, in its classical formulation, was all about the obedient replication of an existing system.

Critical analysts of mentoring programs like de Vries (2011) have proposed that this classical version of mentoring can be distinguished from another form that *could* be used to accomplish a levelling of the gendered playing field. Mentees could, for example, report the conditions of oppression to their mentors. Being senior and successful in institutional terms, mentors could then bring about change on the behalf of mentees. This sounds like an unobjectionable, meritorious idea, and it has been put into practice already. It even has some results to show for itself. Jennifer de Vries, a high-profile mentoring program developer now in private practice, recalled how she initially felt "challenged" by sharp criticisms levelled at women-only mentoring programs by feminist analysts. She remarks:

> [Feminist critic] Anita Devos explored the popularity of mentoring programmes for Australian academic women, and argued that "these programs are supported because they speak to institutional concerns with improving performance in a performance culture, while being seen to deal with the problem of gender inequity" (2008: 195). This highly instrumental approach to mentoring may have very little to do with improving gender equity. As practitioners, Devos challenges us to consider whether WO [women only] mentoring programmes have been co-opted for institutional purposes, at the expense of their broader gender equity goal. While individual women may be assisted to be more successful within the gendered status quo, the overall situation for women may remain unchallenged and unchanged. Despite our good intentions, the gender equity intent may easily be lost (de Vries, 2011: 13).

de Vries responded to these criticisms by developing her "bifocal" approach. One lens is focused on the substantive relations of engagement between senior and junior women in mentoring programs, in which senior women assist their juniors in various ways to develop their academic careers. The other lens is focused on organisational change—on changing the terms of the male dominated game. This dual mandate of substantively developing individual women and bringing about gender equity at the institutional level attempts to avoid the kind of mentoring that inducts women into the conditions of patriarchal power. It attempts to transform mentoring programs from "being a career boost for individuals to an organisational change strategy designed to benefit mentees, mentors and the organisation" (2011: 16).

For de Vries, this is accomplished by means of assigning mentees the task of collecting mentee experiences of the elements of institutional life that oppress and exclude them. Mentors then use that database of knowledge to accomplish institutional change. Educated about the conditions of oppression that may no longer be relevant to or forgotten by those who have become institutionally successful, mentors become change agents for lesser equipped mentees. In deVries's words, mentors are "well placed to act on any increased understanding of gender equity issues that may occur as a result of their mentoring relationships, in order to bring about organisational change" (2011: 16).

To demonstrate how the bifocal approach might be undertaken in and through mentoring programs, de Vries draws on the mentoring component of the Leadership Development for Women program developed and pursued by the University of Western Australia in 1994. As usual, participants in the women-only mentoring program were matched with mentors who were senior to them. Unusually, men were also involved in mentor roles. They were involved at the insistence of the then Vice Chancellor Fay Gale, who took the view that mentoring programs as they stood involved too few senior women who quickly became overloaded with their responsibilities to mentees. Gale wanted to involve senior men who would "own and support" the program (1998: 294). Men needed to be converted to the cause. They were duly enrolled in the program as collaborators in the fight to achieve gender equity in the institution. Gale concluded that this was the way to undergird the importance of mentoring; to recruit senior men to believe in it, and to simultaneously signal its importance to other senior men. If senior men believed in it, and could convert others to this view, broad support and unfurling commitment further up the chain would inevitably ensue.

This rather evangelical approach did indeed change things; of particular note was the vocal support male mentors lent to ongoing funding for the program. Also noteworthy was that the then Deputy Vice Chancellor Alan Robson came to understand that how he ran meetings made it difficult for women to express their views. He changed the meeting format and style, and initiated training for other committee chairs so that a more gender inclusive meeting culture could become normalised. As de Vries herself admits, these are "small wins" (2011: 17), but their collective yield ideally adds up and chips relentlessly away at the conditions of everyday oppression.

As (modestly) successful as such a model might at first seem, irrespective of whether mentors are thought to be facilitating and advancing the careers of mentees, and/or fighting the patriarchy on behalf of mentees, they are located in a hierarchical system of exchange with their mentees. Within it, mentees must take up positions as less equipped parties who require the generosity of relatively better-equipped mentors. Mentors occupy positions that enable them to give; mentees occupy positions of receipt. In such exchange systems, under cover of generosity, mentees become indebted to mentors. We argue that this constitutes a kind of imitation of the patriarchal operations of the university. This is the case even though in de Vries's example, mentees set out what is important to them, *because they still depend on the will of senior others to effect any desired changes.* The changes are small not only because the programs themselves cannot achieve wholesale structural change of the kind that would bring about meaningful institutional gender equity, but also and more importantly because mentors are the embodiment of success that mentees are bidden to replicate. The terms of that success are male. In our analysis, mentoring programs offer us a clear picture of how, effectively, junior women are nurtured into successful senior women—and how those senior women become, in effect, honorary men, such is the result of the embrace they must make of male standards to achieve success. The relations of patriarchal transference thus endure in this systematic approach, and they are obscured by generosity. We think because mentoring programs are specifically charged with bringing junior women to success, the last thing mentoring programs can achieve is wholesale gender equity. It is no mystery to us that the changes that *can* be achieved—changes in the style and form of meetings and the like—are small. And, they depend entirely on the will of good men (and honorary men) to institute.

IMITATIONS

We are deeply interested in imitation in our book; it forms herein a key trope. We will argue that the mentor and the mentee are caught in a system of exchange in which mentor gifts must be repaid by mentees in the same form as they were given. Given, consumed, and repeated are ideas and practices valued institutionally and individually for their utility in gaining purchase in a man's world—chiefly success. Even if we suggested, as de Vries does, that it would be better to have mentees put together a list of how patriarchal structures and practices impact and impede them, mentees and mentors would remain locked in a closed economy of knowledge. The basis of the mentoring relationship is that the mentee does not know of the institution what the mentor knows. The mentor is wiser, more experienced, more practiced; at our own institution, such qualifications are required before a person can become a mentor in the formal program.

The mentee (or the staff member, or the student, or the PhD candidate) can and often does come with views that depart from institutional axiology. As a mentor, Monique, a humanities professor in an Australian university, encountered such departures very frequently. She knew that departures could cause problems. One of her mentees, Cathryn, came to her mind immediately. Cathryn wanted to embark on a program of collective publications with a number of fellow feminist authors, and her five-year plan for publications outputs reflected that intention. Monique thought it admirable, but she knew it would hurt Cathryn's CV. Such a publications program would not let Cathryn evidently "lead"; she would not be able to accrue points against her h-index in the same way she would if she were to publish solo, and in higher-impact journals than she had indicated. It would impede her success. The terms of success are pretty narrowly defined in the neoliberal university, and they require autonomy in the concrete form (in Cathryn's discipline) of single-authored or lead-author publications. So Monique reasoned with Cathryn. She met with her, seeking to undo Cathryn's settled ethical, feminist decision. She succeeded; Cathryn eventually saw its pitfalls as she was engaged in dialogue with Monique. Monique simply questioned, throwing out challenges to Cathryn's plans until Cathryn was sufficiently frustrated to arrive at the conclusion herself that, in the institutional context that would measure and value her outputs, her plan was flawed. She "saw reason," Monique reckoned.

In the neoliberal university, we all tend to do this. We know that students have to demonstrate the learning outcomes we have determined are the most important ones for them to know. We know that we all have to embark on programs of research that will fit particular quality criteria. We know that, as managers, we must produce institutional expectations—meeting targets, goals, budget envelopes. Bringing them about involves us in maieutic methods of sharing and obtaining knowledge. The maieutic method is, essentially, Socratic; a person is engaged in a dialogue by a questioner until frustration caused by challenges to the person's ideas leads him or her to dissatisfaction with his or her settled convictions, and provokes a refinement of his or her views. The presumption is that, really, the mentor, the head of school, the lecturer, already knows what the answer is supposed to be. She leads the dialogue, supplying clues, evidence, indicators to her interlocutor, allowing her to work out what they already know—or what they should know. It is the job of any leader in the current institutional format to allow those farther down the hierarchical scale to work out the predetermined answer. In such operations, the various views that other people hold are valid, even validated; it was not "me" who told another what to think; I only challenged their position, harried it and prodded at it with my superior knowledge of the context that I hold. As the lecturer, the head of school, the expert researcher in a disciplinary field, the mentor, I must, from within the field of knowledge in which I am expert, bring others up. I do not do so by admonishing or undermining their positions, but by questioning their own positions to make sure they, too, can be as successful as I am in the system in which we are both entailed. I listen, I care, I preserve the reality of the other. The philosopher James Freeman puts it this way:

> The challenger exercises a Socratic or maieutic function, drawing out an argument from the proponent as she recognizes that his case presented so far needs further development to constitute a cogent argument or the strongest argument possible (Freeman, 2011: 12).

In this way, we produce replicas of our own successful selves, well within the axiological operational terms of the institution. I might preserve the reality of the other, but I also reduce her because her positions can never disturb me: it is my role to challenge her with my complete and expert knowledge. Her knowledge, however, doesn't impact "me."

This stands for intellectual positions just as much as it does for "leadership" positions, when one can entertain, but not be affected by, the ideas of rivals. This does not mean a person has to accept the ideas of others; we are describing here a kind of knowledge autonomy or intellectual imperialism that can be caring and interested in other's work—but which can never admit their unfamiliar ideas. We all know academics like that. When you go to your next seminar and you can predict the questions that will be asked by each of the assembled senior staff, you know you are witnessing it. Rosalyn Diprose has revealed much about the maieutic conditions afoot in Australian universities. She writes:

> In this exercise of power, there is nothing disturbing, at least not in the end. Hence there is no teaching or learning, no production of new ideas, on such a model. One's mentor, student, companion, or rival is reduced to an intellectual midwife (through the exercise of maieutics), someone who merely helps to brings to consciousness. . . . Philosophical autonomy also describes the paradigm of education currently favored in Australian universities where, under the pressure of economic rationalism, the teacher and the student are reduced to vehicles for the consumption and repetition of familiar ideas valued for their utility in allowing easy appropriation of our world (Diprose, 2000: 124).

What would it take to trouble the production of sameness? The very reproduction of the male-biased institutions as we know them? Institutions feel, in a way, beyond us; they exist as structures bigger and more powerful than the individuals whose lives they array. But critical engagements with them might provoke new understandings of how they might be acted upon. We offer one here, a provocation: that we are all entailed in producing institutional norms. Once we appreciate that these things are created in history or in imaginations in and through the processes we describe in our book, we can potentially act on that understanding. We speculate that such a possibility might arise out of the chaos of COVID-19.

At this point, we offer an example of how the dominant might come to appreciate the suffering of the oppressed—and how things might change as a result.

POSSIBILITIES

Certainly, a lot has changed lately. The exposure of universities to international student markets has, to varying degrees, brought about a major and ongoing financial problem in the wake of COVID-19. Responses to the changes in the financial fortunes of universities have included the cessation of building works, recruitment freezes, the clawing back of forecast travel monies, the initial possibility, and then the grim reality, of staff reductions. An immediate saving was available in the slashing of the casual workforce, upon which the sector has been increasingly dependent for teaching labour since a radical change was made to the relationship between teaching and research in the late 1980s. This "precariat" has suffered greatly as institutions saw little choice but to eliminate casual (mostly sessional teaching) posts in order to secure ongoing academic positions.

While there was outraged protest from ongoing staff members who sought to protect those in the precariat, the conditions under which their protection would be secured also emerged. At some Australian universities, continuing staff members were asked to reduce their dependence on casual academic teaching labour in order to produce a saving to offset some of the losses resultant of the COVID-19 pandemic. The Enterprise Bargaining Agreement (EBA) specifies maximum hours that can be spent in teaching, but many research intensive universities operate much lower hours than the maximum, to protect research productivity. Most continued to do so during the pandemic, but many staff members found themselves with more hours than before. Particularly arduous were making hours, previously allocated to casual staff.

We spoke to some heads of departments who reported complaints from tenured staff about the additional load, often based on how much time mark-ing took up. Yet, casual academic staff were typically contracted to spend about an hour marking the entirety of the assessment items for each student in a humanities or social sciences courses. Prior to the pandemic that had forced the issue, the contributions of casual labourers were forgotten, almost wholly concealed.

But, under crisis conditions, tenured staff members could see that what casual staff actually did was prop up the whole teaching program. What they were recognised for was one hour of marking labour—until there was a crisis that revealed their fundamental importance to the university. Not only did they hold up the teaching program, they permitted tenured staff members to free themselves up to do research; tenured staff could not afford to be spend-ing all of their time on the lesser valued category of teaching. Perhaps for the first time, the real value of casual labour has been realised, and the real con-ditions of their oppression appreciated. Tenured staff have in general thrown their full support behind the precariat. In the school we know of, this support came as a direct result of considering the labour that tenured academic bod-ies would have to endure, even if it was support that came from the horrific realisation of what their own bodies would have to endure as a result of the loss of the casual labour force. We consider the broader possibilities ushered in by the pandemic to consider what else might change in the way of the

appreciation of alterity. We have to remember, though, that whatever appreciation of alterity might arise, casual staff members will suffer like never before
in the stricken university: they have and will likely continue to lose their jobs,
not least because the worst of the economic blow dealt by the pandemic may
be yet to come to the tertiary education sector. We may appreciate their work
more as we bear it on our own shoulders, but it will be knowledge that comes
at their expense. We can hope that when the university invites them back in,
their treatment will be different. Could the same set of possibilities apply to
women? Could women's disadvantage, deeply embedded well prior to, but
made starkly evident by the circumstances of COVID-19, be appreciated in
some new way in the context of the pandemic? We think that the appreciation
of alterity is fundamental to a new understanding of generosity that could
rearrange social imaginaries and their effects—such as "the patriarchy" and
its powerful arraying effects on women and men. It hovers as a possibility,
we suggest.

THE NEOLIBERAL UNIVERSITY?

We've mentioned the neoliberal university several times now. It's an interesting term to use in this context. Neoliberalism is a very well established economic theory that favors free markets and minimal government intervention.
As we explain farther along, that economic theory (itself a fusion of New
Right thinking and neoconservative social philosophy) became dominant
during the Thatcher government of the 1980s, and it remains dominant. We
say it's an interesting term to use in the context of higher education because,
even though state support for the system that had resulted in free education
ended with election of the Hawke government in 1983, it certainly isn't the
case that the higher education system is free of intervention. That has never
been truer than during the COVID-19 pandemic—although Australia's universities would likely prefer that the government intervened in their falling
fortunes rather than doing things like adjusting fees in anticipation of the
post-COVID-19 jobs market. As we point out, those adjustments have seen
humanities and social science degrees increase in cost relative to the STEM
degrees that the Australian government has suggested will be in demand in
the country's near-term economic future. In common with most analysts, we
use the term to denote the sharp pivot away from state responsibility for the
sector to the managerialized system now in place and to the value accorded
knowledge, especially in the export market. While the university is caught
between profit and not-for-profit models and practices, it's fair to say that the
institution is as far removed from a state-supplied service as any other in a
late capitalist context.

This means, too, that it is difficult to speak of "the patriarchy" in terms that distinguish it entirely from capitalist practice. We have just noted that knowledge is valued in economic terms—very highly in Australia's case: it is Australia's third-largest export market (something about which we will say more as our book unfurls). The conditions of valuing knowledge bear with them some important biases, not the least of which is gender. Astute readers will no doubt wonder if they might be able to substitute our term *patriarchy* with *capitalism*. We intend the possibility and invite the reader to ponder what that possibility says about our argument—particularly, its scalability to arenas beyond our own institutional concern in this book.

AN ORIENTATION TO AUTHORSHIP

We have approached this book in a way that departs from most writing partnerships in anthropology, where two equally interested parties with complementary skills produce the work in close collaboration. While we have indeed collaborated on this work, that collaboration is made manifest in a particular way. Ours is a partnership, of equal, but different, contributions. To reflect this, we write as "we," drawing out by name our different contributions where relevant: Alison's as a key informant and Simone's as anthropological analyst.

If we were to use film parlance, we would say that Alison is the star of the show: Alison's experiences appear in all of the core examples or scenes by which we explore mentoring in this book. Being central to each of the scenes, she has been able to make in situ, instantaneous insights of what might be going on. Alison's experiences, though, do not serve as a touchstone against which the experiences of our other 200 interlocutors might be measured, nor do they constitute any kind of measure by which the validity or merit of the analysis made in the book might be tested. Alison is instead a *key informant*.

Like all of our other (200) informants, all of whom are academics employed by universities across the western world, Alison is a participant in the research setting. Unlike them, she has made some analysis of her experiences for this book. And, also unlike them, she has specialist experience that lends her participant contributions special currency and validates her as a key informant. She is distinguished from all other informants appearing in our book because her experiences span most of the elements of our inquiry, as they are represented in our substantive chapter work. Unlike our other informants, Alison can speak across all of the categories of experience upon which our analysis is made. She has been a mentee, and some of her experiences in the institution have been fundamentally shaped by the advice and direction that she received from a formal, named mentor of whom she is very fond. Alison is herself currently involved in a formal mentoring program (at the

ANU) as a mentor. And, Alison is a scientist. She collects and deals with the kind of data that goes through laboratory analysis. Her work as a biological anthropologist working with monkeys living at far remove from our home city of Canberra has been profoundly disrupted by the COVID-19 pandemic, in a way that Simone's work as a social anthropologist working in Australia has not. During the course of writing this book, Alison pursued promotion to her current level of associate professor. Alison has also been accused, if we can put it that way, of being an attractive woman who got her job because of her looks. She has cried at work on several occasions, and she has a young family. She is aware of the ways in which the genderedness of buildings impacts her experience as a woman and a mother and as an academic. She is, as a result of the sum total of her experiences, a longitudinal informant, offering up data at every key point, and experienced in every element of mentoring herein described and analysed. This is, in many ways, Alison's story.

Alison's location at the ANU with Simone has profound implications for the carriage of analysis, not least because it could occur in temporal and spatial immediacy. Alison could provide, effectively, a livestream of data to Simone as events and experiences occurred and, because she is also involved in the crafting of this work, she could not have those experiences without knowing that they might be of value to this research. They also served to emplace our analysis firmly in the context of the Australian National University, which serves as our foundational example throughout.

If Alison is the star of this show, then Simone is the director, analysing Alison's experiences both with her, and beyond her, in specific anthropological terms, to make claims about the social life of the university itself. Simone is not a formal mentor. She has certainly been the recipient of excellent advice from many people, but she has never understood herself as a "mentee," even in retrospect—a consideration she made in the course of writing this book. She has never cried at work, excepting the day she twisted her ankle on a lunch time run, and that, she recalls, was much more "breathless swearing" than it was tearful. She has never been accused of getting her job on the basis of her appearance, which she fervently hopes is because her work is so excellent it's beyond question, rather than because she's deeply unattractive. We will attend, shortly, to the problematic ways in which "attractiveness" is involved in institutional life; even this throwaway, funny line reveals its complex inclusion and how it might be valued and utilised by the self and others at work. Simone used to be mother to a small child, but her son is now an adult. Simone is a member of the professoriate and so, in the words of some of our interlocutors, is "one of the lucky ones," someone who knows "how to play the game" or, in our own terms she is fully "an honorary man." As a social anthropologist who has been deeply interested in the operations of power, and where and how they hide themselves from our view—in this case, in the thick of the generous operations of mentoring programs—Simone crafts the analytic story in which Alison features.

Sometimes, our roles have expanded beyond the parameters we have set out above; we have indicated where this has occurred. This productive relationship permits rich experience to be concurrently twinned with anthropological analysis; there has been no moment, for us, when data has preceded analysis. Our two roles have been inextricably entwined in the sense that we have been able to render simultaneous the acquisition of data and its analysis.

THE STUDY

As we have already noted, this study was conceived in 2018 when we met up for lunch after attending a session provided by the university for mentors it had invited to be part of its formal program. The experience provoked both of us to consider mentoring in a new way, beyond considerations of what kind of mentors we each might make, and under what conditions we would serve as mentors. Our different decisions about involvement in mentoring programs (Alison signed up, Simone did not) and our different, complementary positions, as previously described, allowed us to consider a book-length inquiry.

Our inquiry is confined to women-only mentoring experiences, which are by no means the only version of the practice. Much of what we say will be relevant to general mentoring programs that include men as mentees and mentors, and to other specific programs, such as those pertaining to Indigenous members of the university. We confine our focus to women's experiences for the sake of a producing a well-ordered and clear thesis but we hope that readers will make connections to other relevant areas of mentoring practice. As we have already indicated, and as we describe in the course of this introduction, our definition of mentoring practice spans much more than simply identifiable, named, mentoring programs.

More than this, via the case of mentoring, we aim to offer up a response to the moment that has given us pause to rethink university hierarchy. We wonder what might come of the disruption that COVID-19 has offered up. Among its many disruptions is one that has impacted those who have enjoyed privilege in the knowledge economy, and will perhaps lead to an lived appreciation for those who have been oppressed by it. What will come of this moment? Perhaps nothing will. Yet it offers an invitation to think about its potentials for a different kind of relating between differently privileged bodies in the institution.

An important point to make here is that our interest began in the thick of a mentoring context, so it is an interest born and maintained in the terms of participant observation. We described earlier the key role that Alison plays as participant—as key informant. But we are participant-observers here, too, in the knowledge economy, in the neoliberal university. As our success therein indicates, we are pretty good neoliberal citizens. We make, especially in the period of COVID-19, decisions that serve the best interests of our institution. We are regarded as good economic managers as part of our suite of leadership skills. In that category, we have secured the foundations for teaching quality and its continuation under COVID-19 conditions and endeavoured to safeguard our school's collective research future by designing and investing in research projects that enhance and grow our School's participation in the knowledge economy—in projects that will result in the generation of economic, scholarly, and community benefits. We have regulated teaching hours so that no one's particular shoulders are burdened with too much teaching (and this can be very important to the assurance of gender equity). We have had to hold this success and this participation in critical reflexive regard in order to write this book. This has been very difficult to do, since many of the things against which our own success is measured might be leveraged and pressed into the service of rationalisation. Telling people to be innovative in their teaching, as Simone did almost every day as she balanced the maths and the labour of the school, comes with all the benefits of imaginative invention and all the pitfalls of moulding teaching into the shape of the budget envelope. As head and deputy head of a large school in the university at the time of writing, we have participated in the ways successful women are expected to participate—in recognising hierarchy, in producing savings in difficult times, and in nurturing and growing research activity. We've each produced the performance of success expected of us. But, now, in holding our actions in reflexive regard, in being critical of neoliberal practices, we are embarking on an exercise of some *disobedience*. In so doing, we hope to enliven something from the deep past of university life in Australia, when universities were public—and equipped in true Habermasian style to remark on the conditions in which they were immersed. We want to say plainly here that the university environment in which we live has welcomed our disobedience and embraced what might come of it, with interest, even as the data we draw often comes from direct analysis of this same university's patriarchal practices. There's a lot to be said for a university that supports an investigation of the conditions and presumptions under which daily operations manifest, and it makes for a optimistic work that we hope will expand beyond our local context.

Our study takes in a range of institutions from across the UK, Canada, the US, and Australia within which we accessed both senior academic women mentoring their juniors (a term that may not in fact indicate age seniority) and mentees. We also sourced formal written and verbally expressed ideas about mentoring, about "the patriarchy" and about the institutional positions on gendered participation, which we utilise here. Our mentee and mentor participants completed an initial survey about their experiences of each (and some were indeed included in both surveys, being both mentor and mentee). For those who chose to continue their participation, we conducted an open-ended interview to more deeply explore the kinds of experiences the participants had flagged. We developed an iterative coding system that eventually yielded the main themes we explore in our substantive chapters as they are set out below. Our study took place over twelve months and included a total of 200 participants, all of whom were given pseudonyms; all quotes are attributed to the pseudonym assigned, and provided exactly as our informant expressed their thoughts. We spent in situ time with some of our participants in Australia and overseas, attending to their unspoken demeanours, the spaces in which they were located, the mundane and often overlooked elements of institutional being that yielded such rich results.

As Simone has found in her twenty-year investigation of the governance of tobacco smoking in Australia (see Dennis, 2016), and as Alison has noticed over the course of her career observing the responses primates make to their socio-environmental conditions, there is much to be found in these disattended practices of life in place. We detail our attendances to them, and we link them to the specific chapters that collectively articulate the overarching aim of our book: to get underneath the act of good citizenship that promulgates the corrective technique of mentoring across existing patriarchal structures, undergirding them, and undergirding university hierarchies as it does so.

A final piece of information provides further orientation to our study. Although we have ranged internationally to gather our data, as already intimated, we ground our book in a central focus on our own institution. While we did not seek the participation of colleagues from within our own direct area of management and leadership, women from the ANU did participate in our study; in strict accordance with our ethics clearance for this research, we utilise their information here with their permission. Less evidently, but just as importantly, our own everyday and longitudinal experiences of being at our own institution have informed our findings, as well as furnishing us with practical opportunity to attend public mentoring events. We have additionally accessed the public information that the university has disseminated and that is available beyond communications restricted to institutional members to give especial insights to the context in which we both work and in which mentoring is institutionally supported.

STRUCTURE OF THE BOOK

The first substantive chapter of this book carries on the work begun in this introduction, providing further orientation to the kinds of themes and ideas upon which we most frequently draw with respect to our analysis of mentoring. In this chapter, we describe the role of the Mentor in the Homerian classic. Odysseus's trusted friend guides Odysseus's son, Telemachus, to become a wise leader during the years that Odysseus is engaged in the Trojan War. A much less acknowledged figure, the goddess Athene, or Athena—we use this latter form in this book[2]—is also involved in guiding the young Telemachus to wisdom. While Mentor leads by specific counsel, Athena appears and guides in more figurative ways and forms—often appearing as a bird, a mortal woman, even as Mentor himself, to guide Telemachus. While mentoring programs that bear the name of Mentor appear in our analysis precisely as such, guidance and counsel are given in quite other forms to women in the modern university. Indeed, clues to successful participation, hints as to the state of the patriarchy and one's situation in it, are everywhere to be found, and we have counted them as forms of mentoring, of the kind and form that Athena might have offered in one of her many guises. In the definition of mentoring that we gave earlier in this introduction, we said that mentoring could be defined as any situation in which (in our case) women are led to understand something of their positionedness with regard to "success," and we offered some insight into how it might be achieved, or warned of some impediment that might stand in their way of accomplishing that success. Invoking Athena permits us to think through how advisements are given to women beyond the named programmatic parameters of mentoring.

In this, our work is unique; the analyses that are to be found presently are restricted to describing mentoring as either named formal programs or informal advisement-type relations between two parties (typically, where one party is more senior or experienced than the other). Unusually in this research space, we include the built environs of the university, one-off promotion advisement sessions, and a suite of other examples as properly contained within the realm of mentoring. We attend in this way to Athena's underrecognised and undervalued role in our work as we attend to more versions of mentoring than simply its named versions and forms might permit. But we do not take Athena to be a figure of glorious emancipation for women, or even one who is on their side. Athena was, after all, a protector of kings, and mentoring, in its classical formulation, was all about providing wisdom in a mentee without provoking in them any spark of rebellion. Because we use the figure of Athena to draw out the unseen and largely unrecognised elements of mentoring practice, we provide at the beginning of each chapter a short orientation to how we make figurative use of the goddess therein.

In our second chapter we attend to the conditions of the patriarchy in which mentoring is contextualised. As the scholarly literature clearly indicates, mentoring has been used to furnish women with the skills and capacities to navigate patriarchal institutional circumstances. In 2003, with the publication of Colley's important work, mentoring was revealed to provide the grounds for the rise of a female consciousness based in common grievances against the patriarchy (see Colley, 2003). Colley's insights permitted mentoring to be understood as a weapon in the collective struggle against male privilege, rather than just a wayfinder that could be pressed into the service of navigating a male world. We think, though, that this weapon might have been unintentionally and unknowingly turned inwards, to face those it would seek to emancipate, especially in its imitation of male forms of producing success. We pick this idea up most of all in our fourth chapter, but here we look to the conditions under which imitation might also exist, and permit such forms as we discuss in chapter four to thrive.

With that in mind, in this chapter we track the rise of the university in Australia, noting with especial interest the role of imitation, and the ways in which the patriarchy has changed from outright male privilege to insidious forms of male advantage concealed under cover of neutrality and rationality. We note that (somewhat forced) imitation of government preferences for accountability management, efficiencies and the production of valuable research outcomes made for a wholly remade university sector in Australia (indeed internationally) that has in general disadvantaged female participation beyond certain levels. That is, we argue something is happening once again in Australia as the government takes the opportunity presented by COVID-19 to produce rationalisation in the higher education sector.

Imitation is again a useful trope as we turn to two ethnographically informed examples. In the first, women aspiring to promotion emulate neoliberal presumptions of the standard male figure; in the second, women attempt to have their unique biological and social experiences of life recognised. We pose the argument in this chapter that despite (highly contradictory) appearances of gender neutrality on the one hand, and attempts to cut through gender bias on the other, becoming an honorary man is essential to the accomplishment of institutional success in the forms of promotion and grant application. Both neutrality (often in the form of merit-based ascension, like promotion) and gender bias (such as acknowledging that males are promoted quicker than females) were institutionally recognised in the first ethnographic example, a women-only promotion session, that we examine in this chapter. That contradictory complexity sets the scene for our next chapter, which is given in the form of a very short interlude.

Our third chapter forms an important link between the puzzling contradiction we wind up with in chapter 2 and directly address in chapter four. In this short linking chapter, we speculate on the relationship between transparency and secrets. We think it wise to be wary of the suggestion that what universities say on the one hand, and what they do, on the other, are in opposition. Instead, we think that if we attend closely to the transparent remarks that universities make about gender equity and female participation—and especially about their failings in these areas—we will have no need of going hunting for secrets that undo their claims. We suggest that transparencies are inclusive of all the institutional secrets; they hide in plain sight.

We examine exactly how those secrets hiding in plain sight relate to mentoring in our fourth chapter, arguing that the remarks that institutions make about reflecting gendered participation in built campus environments say all the right things—and simultaneously permit unfettered continuance of patriarchal institutional practice. In this chapter we also demonstrate how institutional involvement in Athena SWAN—ostensibly a transparent move to undermine patriarchal cultures—can also ironically support them.

Between the bold moves to eradicate patriarchy and its demonstrable continuance lies a fertile space for mentoring programs to grow. In the fight against male dominance, so much has been accomplished! There is yet so much to be done! The patriarchy is both dead and very much alive—it is not overt, yet its power remains. We suggest in our conclusion to this chapter that imitation again becomes important. In a liminal period with no clear end in sight, mentoring programs, we argue, have taken up the forms and practices of male dominance that they evidently abhor, in constructing hierarchical relations between senior and junior women.

This hierarchy, we argue in chapter 5, is both enabled and cloaked by the debt relations of generosity. We attend closely to the ways in which modern mentoring programs of the named variety do precisely what the Homerian original suggests they ought: keep things just as they are for the glory of the male master. Arranging junior and senior women into exchange relations of generous giving and hefty, enduring debt, mentoring programs use the tools of the master, so they cannot undo the work of the master. But what could?

In our concluding remarks, we reflect on the ways in which mentoring in all the guises we have examined depends on the production of sameness, the imitation of patriarchal forms, the requirement to make over our junior colleagues in our own image. But we are in unprecedented times. Perhaps such a model will no longer suffice in an environment where the only thing we know is that the university will not be the same as it was before COVID-19. We offer a speculative provocation, around a different version of generosity that values not sameness—but *difference*. Already, it is apparent that different bodies will suffer different fates under COVID-19 regimes; what might be born of this new understanding? Just as we have preceded our analysis of mentoring proper with all manner of questions and contexts, we use it to provoke questions beyond its own operations, probing into a future that none of us can yet know—but about which we may have cause for hope. Unsettlement of the relentless reproduction of patriarchal forms may be in the offing in the form of an equally thickly veiled virus that seems, on the face of it, to bring only more disadvantage to women. But it could surprise us.

NOTES

1. The sandstone universities are typically Australia's oldest tertiary education institutions, generally (but not exclusively) founded in the colonial era. As the moniker suggests, they boast buildings constructed of sandstone. Not all the sandstones belong to the exclusive Group of Eight, which includes some "Red Brick" universities, such as the Australian National University, which were established after the sandstones but before the verdant or gumtree universities that were founded in the 1960s and 1970s. The gumtree universities are located in state capitals and characterised by lush, sprawling campuses. The sandstones nevertheless share in common a student body issuing principally from higher income families and alumni that dominate high income employment and positions of influence.

2. We have elected to use "Athena" rather than "Athene" because the former is likely more familiar to readers, especially in the form of the Athena SWAN program that we discuss later in our book.

Chapter 1

Orienting Concepts and Ideas

This short opening chapter serves as a more substantive introduction to mentoring, and to orient readers a little more to the kinds of concepts and arguments we advance in this book. We take the key features of mentoring that we discuss below out into broader terrains to begin to make our case for using mentoring as a window onto much broader institutional terrains.

PERFECTION

Earlier, we mentioned that the bulk of literature on mentoring has been concerned with its goodness, and we referenced the original Mentor myth; these are intimately connected. The founding principle of mentoring is in part responsible for why mentoring hasn't been rigorously investigated, both in terms of the concept itself, and as a set of resultant ideas and practices. The mentoring concept itself is founded on notions of *perfection* with Homer's epic *The Odyssey* being the most frequently cited original source.

As Colley (2003) notes, academic contributions on mentoring (which are confined to examining named programs and informal person-to-person arrangements) focus either on the figure of Mentor in the epic (e.g., Anderson & Shannon, 1988) or the figure who is disguised as the mentor, the goddess Athena (e.g., Shea, 1992). In the first case, the Mentor possesses truly visionary perception of his ward's true potential and grows it to fruition by acting as the role model who never deviates from the wisest and most advisable path. The ward observes, replicates, imitates, becomes. In the second case, Athena, disguised as Mentor, is the principal figure. As befitting a deity, she is a model of perfection and serves to guide others toward it. These subtleties and analytic preferences aside, it is clear that perfection—in our case in the form of success—is foundational to classical conceptualisations of mentoring.

Perfection is equally writ large in conceptualisations and articulations of contemporary mentoring, particularly as it relates to success. As we will argue throughout this book, the notion of emulating a perfect model of success captures, perfectly, both the concerns that feminist scholars have about the recruitment of women into the dominant conditions of the patriarchy and the tone of the majority of mentoring literature: that mentoring involves the generous donation of senior women's time and effort to bring forward the next generation of successful women.

Alison was the first to be concerned about the performance pressure that modelling perfection would place on mentors, and the burden it would place on mentees as they strove to attain it. As women occupying senior institutional roles, we understand what formal mentoring programs often entail. A common idea that seems to extend across the university context is that senior women have already "made it" and so know the "secret of success." "Participants have also been toldthey know what doesn't work, what fails: you can help others to avoid the pitfalls with the benefit of your own experience."

Alison immediately snappily summarised what she had learned at the session: "Copy exactly what I did if I am a perfect model of success and avoid what I did if I failed." For Alison, the emulation of perfection and the avoidance of anything less than exemplary meant that mentors would have to divide all of their past experience into one or the other form in order to help mentees. Alison, with three children, a husband, two dogs, a pet turtle, a discipline staff, a Deputy Head of School role, a halfway-done grant, many grad students and a headache explained to Simone on the phone while attending to her full laundry basket that she didn't think she could classify things into that particular taxonomy. Simone, with her large industry consultancy, two journal editorships, a large first-year anthropology class, a head of school portfolio, two book contracts, a son who had just purchased a house and was, heartbreakingly, leaving her, a partner also in the employ of the university and a border collie so badly behaved its trainer had moved into the house to deal with it, told Alison that she couldn't either. If she was to, then she'd be that "pitfall" mentor, paraded about as the successful woman whose experiences one would never want to replicate. Her success was real, but it had come at a cost that others would be well advised to avoid. She also said that Alison should probably write a book about the problems associated with either emulating perfection or avoiding pitfall, if she had the time.

Only a short while after Alison had hung up on Simone for making such a ridiculous suggestion, she invited Simone to lunch. After discussing our initial, horrified, reactions to the "perfect models" who allegedly made the best mentors, and deciding the best way of understanding it was by book-length treatment, we reconsidered, much more closely, what perfection might signal.

Simone began to understand, as she collected data and undertook analysis in the service of this book, that perfection could be understood as an index of the relative positions of mentors and mentees, and of men and women. Perfect, infallible performances were extracted from women, lest they appear weak in a male-dominated context. She also became immediately interested in the role of imitation, which forms one stratum of the theoretical bedrock upon which this work rests.

Alison, for her part, understood intuitively that emulation was gendered, and that it meant turning in embodied performances that, for example, rendered tears uncryable at work. It also meant, she knew from experience, accounting for deviations from a standard male trajectory with a curious but precise corporeal mathematics that temporarily excused pregnant, nursing and caring bodies from that male standard, even though on the surface these things looked to be generous concessions. These, Simone realised, were remarks that revealed an exchange, and economy of giving. They were expressions of generous male giving to vulnerable and less able female bodies that arrayed men and women hierarchically: women were permitted leave and license and became resultantly indebted. Often, repayments were made in and through female (maternity, care-giving) absences themselves, where men became the more reliable and present institutional bodies.

Perfect senior female mentors were, as Athena before them, expected to offer their secrets to mentees, but unlike Athena could reap the full measure of benefit from so doing—often in the form of entries on CVs that could be pressed into the service of promotion applications in claims of institutional good citizenship and meaningful service. Mentees, we found, felt keenly the pressure to repay mentors, or pay their gifts forward in a generational pattern of perfection emulation. As we indicated in setting out our argument at the beginning of our introductory chapter, entailment in such indebting, implicitly binding exchanges mimics the hierarchical arraying of men and women in patriarchal institutions.

Finally, we note that the reliance of classical and contemporary mentoring on ideas and practices of perfection have firmly attached themselves to key notions of generosity, particularly in the sense that already perfect women must be truly, perfectly generous to invest their time in those aspiring to become so. It is therefore very difficult to raise critical questions about generosity and success without seeming to attack such laudable qualities. Indeed, mentoring's founding notion of perfection has meant that only certain kinds of questions have been raised and answered about its operations and effects from within the paradigm of mentoring. We step outside the paradigm in order to reconsider them. In so doing, we extend the critical feminist literature that is presently dwarfed by positive assessments of mentoring. But, as we have noted, we also subject that critical feminist literature to scrutiny, thinking as we do that no amount of tweaking will make paradigmatic mentoring programs do anything other than what they presently do: maintain the patriarchal status quo. That line of argument forms the sustaining disquisition of our book. We make it manifest in insights that go deep into the structuring structures of the university itself, meaning that our analysis steps beyond the bounds by which mentoring has previously been encompassed.

Certainly, there is a great deal of scholarship dedicated to how to carry mentoring out to best effect—a literature, in other words, that does not challenge or critically investigate the foundational goodness of mentoring, but which serves only to assess quality of practice and efficacy within that paradigm (Merriam, 1983: 169–170; Gulam & Zulfiqar, 1998:4). Stepping beyond this literature permits important ideas to emerge about mentoring's conceptualisation, its entwinement with the knowledge economy in which the neoliberal university is now deeply entailed and its relationship to their patriarchal power structures.

THE PATRIARCHY

As we have indicated, in our book we attend specifically to the relationship between mentoring and the patriarchy. It is worth drawing this out just a little here, forward of our fulsome treatment of it, to introduce several other intertwined ideas that form part of the theoretical underpinning of this work.

For the bulk of analysts, mentoring is intended to serve as a corrective to the incontrovertible facts of male dominance across the sector and is used in the service of everything from effecting change in the dominance of males in prestige positions to raising the status of women in male-dominated research areas, to correcting expressions of enduring sexism. As is broadly the case across political and business contexts, the contemporary university is deeply concerned with equal female participation across the institution and now, it seems, is especially concerned with supporting women's participation in leadership roles. Across the Western world, snapshot reports and longitudinal studies indicate the tenacious grip of male dominance in such roles. In 2016, this principal longstanding explanation for its enduring hold was declared to be myth. In that year, the American Council on Education (ACE) Centre for Policy Research and Strategy and its Leadership Programs Division released a joint report that updated key statistics about women in higher education (Johnson, 2016). It closely examined issues such as tenure, and representation in high-ranking leadership positions. The report, entitled Pipelines, Pathways, and Institutional Leadership: An Update on the Status of Women in Higher Education, was part of the Higher Education Spotlight series, which in turn traces its genesis to The White House Project: Benchmarking Women's Leadership, published in 2009 (Johnson, 2016). Back then, the paucity of female leadership was taken to be an issue of "the pipeline"—the notion that too few women were qualified to enter leadership roles. In the 2016 report, though, key data showed very clearly that women were, in fact, moving unimpeded through the pipeline and being prepared for leadership positions indeed, at a far greater rate than were men—and they were doing so across the board. Female students were revealed to have earned half or more of all baccalaureate degrees for the past three decades and half of all doctoral degrees for almost a decade. Women were trained and ready, even at the very earliest stages of their careers, to move ahead. But despite the number of female graduates available for leadership positions, women were found in the report not to hold associate professor or full professor positions at anywhere near the same rate as their male peers. The pipeline, in other words, appeared to have a serious blockage.

The report then turned to detail the nature of the blockage, finding male faculty members held a higher percentage of tenure positions at every type of institution, even though they did not hold the highest number of faculty positions at every rank. Put more bluntly: the more prestigious the position, the fewer the number of female faculty who had tenure. The report's information brief also found a persistent, tenacious pay gap; during the 2013–2014 academic year, male faculty members made an average of USD$85,528, and female faculty members made an average of USD$70,355. No matter the academic rank, men made more than women and were more likely to hold a tenured or tenure-track position. The picture remained similarly bleak at leadership levels for both administrative and academic roles. The report and its appeal to corrective action stands metonymically for the state of gendered affairs across the university sector in the West.

The ACE's Division of Leadership Programs immediately commenced work on unblocking the pipeline, releasing its "Moving the Needle" initiative. The national call-to-action campaign is a corrective to gender bias, placing the responsibility for the lack of female participation in all levels at the top. It asks presidents of colleges, universities and related associations to commit to helping achieve the goal that by 2030 half of US college and university chief executives are women. This requires institutions to be alive to the issue and demonstrate structural willingness to correct it by privileging qualified women over men where appropriate. It also recognises that women need to look to those few who *had* accomplished success on the same level as men. Mentoring is an obvious and immediate solution to the issue. It is presently entailed in intricate and remedial desires and practices regarding destabilising the foundations of patriarchal dominance (Johnson, 2016). It might not be able to do that, we argue.

One of the early signals of its failure to do so was revealed in how motherhood is depicted in conversations about the patriarchy. In her 1974 work now regarded as a disciplinary classic, Sherry Ortner published her breakthrough article "Is Female to Male as Nature Is to Culture?" She substantiated an explanatory analysis pivoting on a binary framework that attributed women's status to a closeness with nature, and men's with culture and "higher" human activities. Here is a problem: the devalued association of women with nature renders the task of "elevating" women to a level equal with men especially difficult because of the reality of female biology and the perceived universality of male dominance. This problem is certainly recognised in the university complex; the unevenly distributed burden of birthing and care is "a career disruption" that must be rendered visible, comprehensible, explicable, to (both male and female) assessors of promotion applications and grants proposals. But making these labours visible precisely as a kind of "hold up" has amplified debates about what keeps women from excelling in the patriarchal system, rather than consistently quelling them.

Here is another problem: neutrality plays a role here, too, often alongside the recognition of gender-specific biological and sociological labours. As Vu and Doughney (2007) remark, these two things are often brought into concert in highly consequential contexts, such as promotion rounds. In their 2007 work, they found that even though equal merit among men and women in the promotional applicant pool was generally observed, problems nevertheless arose when the subtleties of gender disadvantage were not taken under consideration. In their view, selection panels "become insensitive to gender inequality and discrimination in the social distribution of the responsibility for care precisely when sensitivity is needed most" (2007: 64). Perhaps it ought not be a surprise then, that many women we interviewed thought that if they engaged in nurturing and reproductive labour, they might actually be playing into regressive, patriarchal stereotypes that maintain bondage—even though, ostensibly, there existed institutional means to express what that labour meant in context.

We found, too, the idea that the university's attempts to poke at the patriarchy could be interpreted as imposing on women participants a combative gendered stereotyping that flattens out differences among women in favour of clearly marking and extending the differences between women and men; and to hand women and men an identity that is symbolic, timeless, and archetypal. For those who saw things this way, the development of a specific individuality unique to each researcher became impossible to articulate to a roomful of promotions assessors capable only of seeing the triumph of the woman in a man's world. The complications kept coming. What if a woman didn't want to have children? Would she be viewed as less accomplished and less triumphant relative to colleagues with kids? Would she have had sufficient outputs to overcome, enough to balance the books, if compared? Would she be judged like a man? What if one did want to have kids? When would be the best time to be "disrupted"? And as for men, would their parental labour ever count inside the bubble of the matriarchy myth? These kinds of questions of course buy directly into the model we mentioned earlier—the model of the successful woman who triumphs despite hardships. We do not stay with pregnancy and maternity as our key examples; we move into space (university geographies and buildings) into matters temporal (the development of research and teaching values over and in time)—and embodied experience to give insight into the devaluing of alterity to make our claims.

PARADIGMATIC MENTORING

The literature on mentoring overwhelmingly promotes its benefits. The fact that mentoring programs are routinely presented in positive terms effectively disguises or consigns to the shadows those effects not considered laudable, or even admissible—such as the idea that mentoring programs may not consistently serve the interests of their female participants, as many feminist scholars have noted (see e.g., Acker, 1990; Devos, 2004; Cockburn, 1991; and Colley, 2003). We dig deeper, beyond the feminist critique, to demonstrate the ways in which "good" mentoring yet sustains hierarchical, patriarchal relations.

Mentoring is frequently described as a special kind of community that itself begets and builds community. The following excerpt from Art of Mentoring, an Australian-based international specialist mentoring firm, makes the point explicitly; the term *community* and the term *mentoring* are constant companions:

> a good mentoring program is inexorably linked to community, both feeding an organisation's sense of community and drawing on community to bolster the mentoring relationship. Mentoring programs foster community (Art of Mentoring, 2020).

This view persists in institutional descriptions of "mentoring communities," in the views of our interlocutor, too. At our own institution, mentoring is described not only as an expression of the university community, but as a gateway through which it might be entered. "Mentoring makes for an extended family," proclaims one 2019 ANU News page, inviting others to enter it (see Australian National University 2019c). It is, equally, described as a generator, a builder of community, as well as being, in and of itself, an enclosed learning and support community, as it is at numerous other institutions, both private and public. Of interest to us here is that the paradigmatic enclosure of mentoring within an envelope of "good" bears a strong resemblance to the study of communities.

As a component, a fosterer of, a gateway into or a community in itself, we think it is likely the case that mentoring has been understood in the consistently positive terms in which community has also been understood. It is worth drawing this out a little, to appreciate the positive enclosure of analysis in which mentoring and community are each contained—a containment that has had enduring effect on how community and mentoring are understood.

Community Studies[1] conceptualises community as an ideological discourse that mitigates conflict, so conflict is subsumed under the capacity of community to ameliorate any dispute. Difference and conflict are wholly encompassed within the conceptual embrace of "community," rendering them intrinsic problems within bounded localities that "community" itself exists to address. This understanding of conflict emerged from Max Gluckman's seminal and enduring definition of community as "a lot of people co-operating and disputing within the limits of an established system of relations and cultures" (1958: 35n1). Community is equally conceptualised as "multivocal" (Cohen, 1985), a symbol sufficiently nebulous as to enable its members to hold entirely different views about what "it is" while simultaneously believing that they are sharing something entirely identical. In British Community Studies in general, community is conceptualised as an homogenous, or unitary, social artifact (Agrawal & Gibson, 2001: 9–10). This defining feature of British Community Studies is the principal reason for another founding conceptualisation: the inextricable intertwinement of community with goodness (Williams, 1976: 76). As Watts (2000) argues, the core conceptualisation of community as both something "good" and as a "unity as an undifferentiated thing . . . that speaks with a single voice," has lent community "intrinsic powers" that mute a multiplicity of differences and conflicts and inhibits further conceptual innovation (2000: 13).[2]

We are especially interested in this history of community studies because its history of conflict amelioration, its memorialisation of dominant members and its obscuration of disadvantaged members bear distinctive parallels to the rise of mentoring. Especially pertinent to our work here is the enclosure of both community and mentoring within an envelope of "goodness." As is the case with respect to community, the enclosure of mentoring within this envelope of goodness makes it difficult to raise critical questions about it.

We certainly experienced this difficulty ourselves. In the course of our research, we reviewed reports on mentoring programs on the ANU News pages. One in particular stuck in our minds. It included the following passage:

> The number one benefit for mentors is the capacity to give back . . . . You might not always think you can give something back but based on the experiences of mentees and the feedback they give us we know they are incredibly grateful for the advice, consideration and support that they receive from each of the

mentors. So there is a bit of a heart-warming experience in giving something back to the next generation of future women leaders. Just seeing how the next generation of females is actually shaping up is something that's pretty incredible and having a hand in that is also heart-warming as well (Australian National University, 2020).

These are very obviously genuinely felt sentiments, and there is no disputing that the mentees gave positive feedback on the mentoring that they received as part of the program. This was, no doubt, a good, lovely, positive event. How is it possible for us to cast it in any other light?

As we have said, it is very difficult to critically investigate laudable activities. But our intention here is not to call genuinely felt sentiments into question. We attend, instead, to the recurrent theme arising in this and the other descriptions of mentoring: the goodness of mentoring arises from its key activity—senior women *giving* to their juniors the benefit of their experience and knowledge. In the above excerpt, we note that the phrase "giving back" is used. This we heard many times from mentors and mentees alike. Mentors used the phrase to express their own indebtedness to those who had supported them in their pursuit of success and to pay that debt forward to the next generation of young successful women in the making. Mentees used it to express their debts to present mentors. Indebtedness and giving cycled in and through descriptions of mentoring, and it is to this consistently arising theme that we attend.

A pernicious benevolence of mentoring emerged when we realised the frequency of reference to *giving* in our interviews with mentees and mentors, and its structuring properties that arrange mentors and mentees in hierarchical relation to one another. Statements about giving led us to question the taken-for-grantedness of apparently paradigmatic phrasing. Little (1990) addresses this sinister side by launching a scathing critique on the goodness of the Mentor himself and, by extension, the mentoring programs that bear his name.

In 1990, Little issued an important caution, one that we underscore here. Little noted that in the light of the extent of mentoring practice, the volume of empirical inquiry about it is small: "rhetoric and action have outpaced both conceptual development and empirical warrant" (297). Little noted, too, that the development of theoretical approaches to mentoring are important for getting to the heart of what mentoring accomplishes in the institution, purposively and in unintended ways. This is especially because mentoring seemed to her to be approached with a kind of manic optimism.

Little's insight remains as relevant today as it was three decades ago: the paucity of analysis in this area remains. Instead, works focussed on the form of mentoring have proliferated. The questions of these commentaries included:

what kind of mentoring works best? Gender specific? Intradisciplinary? Formal? Informal? External programs provided by experts? Internal ones that tap into the individual successes within the institution? Parallel mentoring between colleagues at the same level? An approach that combines some of these elements? These kinds of inquiries continue the explosion of activity that began in the business world in the 1970s, where, as Roche noted in 1979, mentoring had established its reputation as a practice that could play a vital role in the development of corporation executives. In Australian universities, formal mentoring programs became popular in the 1990s, coincident with the rise of neoliberalism.

This is not to say that mentoring has no theoretical basis—indeed it makes constant recourse to a single classical conceptualisation that emerges from Homer's *Odyssey* (by no means exhaustively, this list includes Anderson & Shannon, 1995; Bushardt et al., 1991; Carruthers, 1993; Donovan, 1990; Daloz, 1983; Field & Field, 1994; Jarvis, 1995; Kalbfleisch & Keyton, 1992; Little, 1990; Meginnson & Clutterbuck, 1995; Monaghan & Lunt, 1995; Murray, 1991; Parsloe, 1995; Shea, 1992; Smith & Alred, 1993; Stammers, 1992; and Tickle, 1993).

Homer's *Odyssey* provides a narrative that apparently defines and elaborates the qualities of contemporary mentoring and raises enduring questions of how these qualities can be best developed and leveraged in mentoring programs and practices. The presence or absence of such qualities are marshalled to identify what is required for a woman to move up the ladder by way of generally performing better on all the key markers against which academic achievement is judged. This might include publishing more, generating a resultantly impressive h-index, developing networks by recognition of reputation. In and through them, a higher and better recognised profile might be generated. Mentees might be counselled to develop a particular identified quality or expand another. The upshot is that the qualities embodied in the figure of Homer's Mentor can guide contemporary mentors, who are understood to embody them to shepherd mentees on an upward trajectory through the institution.

The paradigmatic narrative goes like this: the caring and shepherding practice of mentors is designed to convey those at the bottom to the top. It produces a gendered change in how the top looks and effects institutional change because those at the top do not protect their own privileged positions; instead they beneficently invest in the positions of others. This beneficence has the net effect, so the narrative goes, of flattening the institutional hierarchy. Beneficence raises women up: self-interest is converted to the collective interests of the marginalised. Pfund, Branchaw, Hurtado, and Eagan (2016) note for example that learning outcomes and accomplishments and research productivity rise for women and minorities to institutional benefit as a result of mentoring:

> Strong mentorship has been linked to enhanced mentee productivity, self-efficacy, and career satisfaction; it is also an important predictor of the success of researchers in training. Students who are mentored report fewer academic non-persistence decisions with positive mentoring being cited as the most important factor in degree attainment. Mentored graduate students and junior faculty are more likely to publish their research than counterparts who are not mentored. Those with mentors also express more confidence, report experiencing higher career satisfaction, and feel greater support for their careers than their peers without mentors. Mentorship positively impacts not only the mentee but also the mentor. Though there is less research about the benefits of being a mentor, increased productivity among research mentees inevitably leads to increased productivity for research mentors (Pfund et al., 2016: 238).

More generally (i.e., not in specific respect of women or minorities) van der Weijden, Belden, van Arensbergen, and van den Besselaar (2014) assert that those who receive mentorship,

> have a more positive view on their work environment and manage their research more actively. Furthermore, young professors with a mentor on average perform better in terms of acquired grants. These findings indicate that it is important for universities to actively organize mentorship programs for young senior staff (2014: 275).

Is there more going on in Homer's *Odyssey*? Can generosity and beneficence have perverse effects? On the hunt for more, we return to Homer.

FOUNDATIONAL QUALITIES OF THE MENTOR

Anyone interested in learning anything about mentoring will simultaneously get a lesson on Homer's epic poem about the adventures of Odysseus, the King of Ithaca. Centrally involved therein is Mentor, the old, wise and trusted sage who was charged with the care of Odysseus's son Telemachus, while Odysseus fought in the Trojan war. Mentor was also assigned the role of advising and serving as guardian for the whole Royal household (see Anderson & Shannon, 1995: 25). The many contemporary commentators on mentoring we listed above draw out some aspects of Mentor's qualities but neglect others. This partiality is telling. Roberts (1999: 81) notes, critically and suspiciously, the endurance only of Mentor's "admirable qualities of counsellor, teacher, nurturer, protector, advisor and role model." Carruthers

(1993: 9) adds that "Mentor had to be a father figure, a teacher, a role model, an approachable counsellor, a trusted adviser, a challenger, an encourager." Little (1990: 298) ascribes Mentor "the full measure of wisdom, integrity and personal investment."

Possessed of these qualities and intentions, Mentor discharged his *nurturing* duty to Telemachus. Mentor's duty was to "draw forth the full potential in Telemachus." Telemachus would then respond well and willingly to Mentor's advice. Mentor's task was "*intentional*" in the sense that his counsel was designed to accomplish something at its conclusion—namely for Telemachus to "*grow in wisdom **without** rebellion*" (Anderson & Shannon, 1995: 25–26, our emphasis; see also Clawson, 1980).

By contrast Roberts questions these sorts of paradigmatic assumptions to reveal the multiple ways in which Mentor "largely failed in his duties of keeping the King's household intact" (1999: 84). Roberts's analysis yields two important insights. The first draws attention to the role of Athena, the goddess who also dispensed advice to the young ward. She took a number of forms to do so, including Mentor's own form. Intriguingly, this female figure is consistently overlooked in the contemporary mentoring literature. It focuses instead squarely on Mentor as the male figure who possesses all the qualities that bear his name in contemporary mentoring praxis. Roberts, by recourse to Klein (1967: 964), analyses Mentor's name: *Men* is "one who thinks"; *tor* is its masculine suffix. Mentor then, is a man who thinks. But perhaps Mentor would have been better called Men*trix*, a woman who thinks, given Athena's role in the dispensation of nurturance and guidance to Telemachus. The bulk of the works taking readers back to a founding conceptualisation of mentoring fail to mention that it was the goddess Athena, goddess of the strange dyad, war and wisdom, who took Mentor's form, along with others, such as a seagull, a ship captain's daughter, a pitcher-bearing girl, a tall, beautiful and accomplished woman, and a swallow so as to counsel and guide both Odysseus and his son Telemachus (Rieu, 1946). The overlooked female operating behind the fully recognised and memorialised male façade of Mentor is certainly not lost on us as we write a book about mentoring in an historically patriarchal institution. Ideas about who is memorialised in the act of mentoring are important to our central thesis, and we return to them throughout this work. That she is overlooked does not mean we see Athena as the heroine of gender equity. Indeed, in our fifth chapter, we suggest that just as Athena stepped into the role of the male Mentor to create wise obedience in Telemachus, successful women, made so by their mastery of the male institutional game, similarly create wise obedience in their junior charges.

Still, in our view contemporary commentaries construct a dominating male façade of Mentor that effectively screens the dynamic role of a female in the classical narrative. This points to the conundrum with which contemporary mentoring practice wrestles, and that feminist analysts have specifically addressed—how, in an historically patriarchal institution, can women be brought out of the institutional shadows and into rising success? These kinds of questions involve the declaration of mentoring as "good" or "bad" and have raised further questions for analysts about how to bifurcate the dual propensities of mentoring programs to serve the interests of the patriarchy and provide women with tangible career benefits.

De Vries (2011) has been particularly interested in extracting the positive elements and jettisoning the negative. As we noted in our introduction, the assignation of "goodness" to some elements of mentoring makes it hard to assess resultant programs in anything other than positive terms. We attend to that difficult task in chapter five, cutting through a tough outer shell of beneficence and generosity. It is, as we show in that chapter, very difficult to critique *generosity,* but our analysis of "good" mentoring forms demonstrates that these forms can have serious effects on the accomplishment of gender equity. It can even replicate the patriarchal power structures that keep women institutionally oppressed.

Roberts's second point concerns the ascription of the qualities of mentoring to the French writer and educationalist François Fenenlo, and his novel of instruction *Les Adventures de Telemaque*. Roberts argues that it is in fact in this work that "one finds the Mentor whose attributes, functions and behaviours [that should] have become synonymous with the modern-day usage of the term mentor and the action of mentoring. Recognition of Fenenlo's Mentor, as opposed to Homer's minor character, Mentor, is called for" (1999: 84).

Interestingly, none of the paradigmatic qualities assigned mentoring from a founding conceptualisation change in the slightest in their ascription to Fenenelo instead of Mentor. Rather, the dominance of these qualities remains, whomever one picks as the best candidate. In Roberts's view, Fenenlo succeeds where Mentor fails. Roberts's guiding questions ask how well each figure did at discharging his duty. Roberts asks (and responds emphatically in the negative):

> was the original Mentor wisdom incarnate? Did he guide, counsel, advise, and enable the young Telemachus? Was a supportive, nurturing and intentional process evident within Homer's writings? Did Mentor "keep everything intact" as instructed by Odysseus? (1999: 82).

We think this is a really good illustration of the contemporary mentoring paradigm, in which the only real question raised is how *effective* a mentor is at mentoring. Clearly Roberts thinks Mentor was pretty poor at discharging the duties left to him by Odysseus, and that instead Fenenlo's name should be synonymous with mentoring practice (quite aside from the fact that Mentor effectively claimed the good work he did do when really, this work was done by a woman hidden from our view by the much better recognised man). But nowhere in the argument about who is the better mentor amongst the two male figures on offer *is the goodness of mentoring itself called into question.*

BENEFICENT MENTORING

Our take on the underlying paradigm of contemporary mentoring is readily confirmed by an exploration of the voluminous literature on the topic. This was summarised by granular work undertaken by Meschitti and Lawton-Smith in 2017. In their comprehensive review, four main topics are identified in the field covering (1). the mentee's perspective and mentoring outcomes; (2). the mentors' perspective; (3). group and multiple mentoring as a strategy for fostering support and networking and (4). mentoring women as a resource for fostering institutional change (2017: 173). They note of these categories a clear underlying shared beneficence:

> in the first case, mentoring is beneficial because it has positive effects for the mentee (this is the most recurring topic); in the second, the mentor role is particularly relevant for a good mentorship; in the third, a move from the dyadic to the group relationship is beneficial; in the last, that mentoring should be used to change institutions [for the better] (173–174).

The strength of the paradigmatic "goodness" and beneficence of mentoring is here already clearly evident, but Wilson and Elman (1990) noted at the time that what *was not* present in a list of beneficial outcomes of mentoring is the benefit that mentoring delivers to institutions. Institutional benefit has since become important to arguments about the worth of mentoring programs (see for example de Vries, 2011). Wilson and Elman argue that these might include:

> the long-term health of the organization as a social system . . . mentoring provides a structured system for strengthening and assuring the continuity of organizational culture. The existence of a strong corporate culture that provides members with a common value base, and with implicit knowledge of what is expected of them and what they in turn can expect from the organization, can be vital to organizational success and effectiveness. The mentoring system is also useful when the organization requires modification or redefinition of culture, i.e., during times of leadership succession. The alternative in many cases is to rely solely on an expensive, intrusive, and highly formalized monitoring and control system. Mentoring can thus be used as an adjunct to the typical

performance appraisal and salary-based sources of information about how well one is doing in the system (1990: 90).

On the face of it these institutional benefits might seem innocuous enough, but recall what Homer's Mentor was expected to produce in the young Telemachus: he was to "grow in wisdom *without rebellion*" and to "*keep everything intact*" (Anderson and Shannon, 1995: 25–26, our emphasis). This alerts us that one benefit that institutions might reap could be keeping things just as they are while equipping individuals to better navigate the hierarchical, patriarchal institution *as it stands*. The possibility that the patriarchal structure of the institution might be preserved despite or even because of the shepherding of mentees upward within the university's structure is not generally contemplated in the existing literature. This task is left to feminist scholars, who immediately assign it a negative value. The claim that mentoring will flatten institutional hierarchies for women, a clear claim of the contemporary mentoring literature, is otherwise taken for granted. Focussing on how effective mentoring is, the current literature sidesteps the possibility that mentoring *supports* the hierarchical arrangements of the university.

When it is addressed in critical feminist analysis, another side-step is made, as we point out in what follows.

BENEFICENT MENTORING?

Those of us in the academy are acutely aware of the multiple ways in which university hierarchies arrange our work. This is a function of the involvement of universities in the knowledge economy that has standardised performances. Many of us, for example, hold an ambition to produce a research reputation with an impressively high h-index that ranks us relative to our contemporaries. Elite institutions are bound up in finding advantageous positions in international ranking performances. Mentoring serves as a course of action to secure quality performance—it is in the interests of the institution to invest in junior researchers for the assurance of high performance in the future, as Wilson and Elman (1990) plainly argue. But there are other manifestations of hierarchy that concern the kinds of stories that institutions tell themselves about themselves—and that they require their members to understand and promulgate. It is here that mentoring may be entailed with the hierarchical arrangement of the institution. The following excerpt, expressed as a benefit that corporate entities might reap from investing in formal mentoring programs is illustrative:

Just as in traditional societies where tribal folklore and fables, each of which contains a "moral," are passed down from generation to generation, mentors in corporate cultures can pass down organizational folklore and fables. The culture-carrying myths and legends may be passed along without mentors, but a mentoring program can reinforce the diffusion process. Mentors can be trusted sources who lend credibility to these cultural stories. They can also put organizational myths in perspective and enlighten junior members as to their deeper meanings. This context-providing function can be especially important for myths which may reflect the less positive aspects of the organization's culture, such as units with ruthless top management. Such negative myths are never written down, but are often joked about. In addition to being transfer agents of corporate culture, mentors also provide immediately practical services for their mentees. Such diverse "services" as informing their proteges of the best ways to navigate the subtleties of the organization's informal political system, acting as a sounding board for ideas with which a junior colleague might be hesitant to approach a supervisor, and even providing mundane advice about appropriate styles of dress, all fall within the purview of mentoring. It is clear that mentors serve as nodes in an information transmission network (Wilson & Elman, 1990: 89).[3]

The operation of organisational myths and the arraying of institutional members in relation to them is alarming especially because mentoring itself can be regarded as an element in undergirding, preserving and future-proofing myths. That is, mentoring is now thoroughly institutionalised and can play a key role in the promulgation of hierarchical arrangements that ensure the very female dispossession and disempowerment it ostensibly addresses. Here we find exactly the qualities so lauded in Homer's Mentor: he would nurture to draw forth the full potential in the mentee, who would "respond well and willingly" to his advisements and "grow in wisdom without rebellion" (Anderson & Shannon, 1995: 26). Mentees would participate positively, and without rebellion, in the conditions of their own domination by learning how to play the game and internalising and embodying the organisational myths that contain the core values of the institution. We note that the core qualities of Mentor might be put to the greatest benefit to keeping the institutional power relations wholly *intact*—another key accomplishment expected of Mentor in his classical depiction (Anderson & Shannon, 1995).

This shepherding of mentees into institutional culture that we have just described jars with the presumption that the organisation invests in mentoring solely for the benefit of the mentor and mentee. It is the beneficence of the mentor–mentee relationships that is the predicate of the literature on mentoring, even though mentoring is also always assigned antidotal properties that would recognise and correct "the main factor making mentoring for women important in universities: that academia has been always been a male dominated environment" (Meschitti & Lawton-Smith, 2017: 171; see also van den Brink & Benschop, 2014; Savigny, 2014; Quinlan, 1999; Bagihole & Goode, 2001).

A case in point is that produced by Gardiner, Tiggemann, Kearns, and Marshall who in 2007 undertook a comprehensive survey of mentors and mentees at Flinders University that included a control group of women who did not receive mentorship. The aim of the survey was to get past the notion that mentorship was somehow simply "good" and to prove that this was *empirically* the case. The survey showed clearly that women who received mentoring did much better on a range of performance measures compared with their unmentored counterparts. What is striking about this study is its narrowness and its adherence to the contemporary form of the original mentoring myth: the conclusion is that women performed better at producing all of the outcomes valued by the patriarchy. Studies conducted within a similarly narrow set of parameters abound and are in the vast majority (see for example, Bell, Golombisky, Singh & Hirschmann, 2000).

Some feminist analysts (de Vries, 2011; Devos, 2008) *have* taken issue with the "goodness" of mentoring and attempt the work of explicating the political institutional contexts in which mentoring is undertaken. As Devos (2008) notes in her examination of the exponential growth of mentoring programs that have flourished in the neoliberal institutional environment of Australian universities over the last three decades:

> these programmes are [institutionally] supported because they speak to institutional concerns with improving performance in a performative culture, while being seen to deal with the problem of gender inequity . . . mentoring [must be analysed in accordance with its location] within a network of institutional power relations, in so doing unsettling the truths we hold about mentoring as always good and unproblematic . . . [so doing] offers an important account of why mentoring has become so popular in these places in these times and reflects on the implications for feminist political goals. . . . Mentoring simultaneously offers a set of technologies for regulating behaviour and promoting self-regulation by women within the performative cultures of their institutions. . . . Mentoring then, is both concerned with improving performance, and implicated in the task of governing performance in accordance with institutional norms. It can hence be both enabling and constraining for women in bringing about personal or institutional change (195).

Analysts following Devos have attempted to cleave the "enabling" elements of mentoring (career development, participation in expanding networks of scholars, and so on) often with the expressed view of extricating mentoring programs from those relations with the institution that would result in female co-option into the patriarchy (see de Vries, 2011). Throughout our book, we deploy the term "enabling mentoring" to denote the "good" bits of mentoring that de Vries distinguishes from the "bad" induction of women into the patriarchy. While such attempts recognise the paradigmatic enclosure of mentoring as good and purposefully step beyond it, another feature of mentoring programs that continues to entangle women in patriarchal relations remains overlooked. The versions of mentoring that analysts like de Vries extract (its "enabling" features that concern career development and beneficial networking) appear on the face of it to, indeed, be "good." They are, however, entailed in the hierarchical relations of giving; the generous gifts of mentors result in the allocation of debt for mentees.

The work undertaken by feminist theoreticians like de Vries (2011) and Devos (2008), among other feminist theoreticians, is extremely significant insofar as subjecting mentoring to fulsome critical examination is concerned. We seek, however, to put that critical work under the microscope in this book by attending specifically to the relations of giving that are fundamental to the "good" mentoring programs that feminist critics advance.

GENEROSITY

A key undergirding of our book, and most especially of our fifth chapter where we explore named mentoring programs, is the complex of relations and practices of generosity and giving. Unlike the historical conceptualisation of mentoring, giving has *not* been theorised as essentially good. An emphasis on the relations of giving help us to look beyond ostensible positivity of giving to another person, to the hierarchical relations that underpin giving. In our conversations and correspondences with them, our interlocutors very frequently referenced the generous giving of mentoring. They described the terms of their engagement with one another, and the positions they occupied as individual members of a structured system of giving and receiving.

Analysis of this data reveals the high importance attributed to generosity by our informants. It reveals, too, that generosity was expected to be repaid by mentee recipients. We apply Marcel Mauss's seminal understanding of the gift economy, set out in his 1925 text *The Gift*, to understand the cycle of giving and indebtedness in which mentors and mentees are involved. So doing allows us to critically question "generosity" and to reveal mentoring relationships as deeply powerful and hierarchically arranged relationships.

Mauss initiated the notion that giving, rather than commodity transaction, establishes communal relations. His is an argument about a gift-based social economy, an economy that might be hidden under the pretense of equal social contracts between individual agents. The gift from one community member to another determines not only what might appear to be the preexisting identity of the individual, but equally their rank and situation relative to others—givers and receivers are made. Gift givers are morally privileged over gift receivers and concurrently with the gift itself receive a moral obligation to give back to the giver: giving distributes to each party the reciprocal relations of obligation. This obligation cannot be repaid in any terms other than by the maintenance of a social bond (Mauss, 1925: 6). The especial power of the gift to make and maintain social bonds arises from its spiritual status: the transfer of a possession is part of the personhood of the giver.

This notion puts Mauss's thesis beyond that of the social contract theorist. While social contract theorists do assume that a part of one's personal property is exchanged through contract, they consider the exchange of a commodity essentially separate from the self. Mauss assumed that the gift remains part of the personhood of the giver, conferring on the recipient the obligation to reciprocate. Thus, the capacity to build a community based on entailed, personal obligation is created. This model of social exchange is not constituted by the exchange of a commodity (whether thing, skill or knowledge) deemed separate from the self but precisely because the gift embodied part of oneself given to another. Further, the respective identities of the giver and the recipient are not given in isolation prior to the giving of the gift; what is constituted through the gift is the social identity of each in relation to the other. Because the gift constitutes the social identity of the parties and with it an enduring social bond that obligates the recipient to the donor, the debtor in this exchange is the recipient, rather than the giver—another contrast with the contract model of social exchange.

Mauss's model reveals how people might be entailed with one another sufficient to form a community beyond the social contract and reveals the hierarchical arrangement of such a community. If one follows the classical Maussian thinking, there are three moral grounds for economic relations: communism, exchange and hierarchy. As David Graeber explains,

> Everyday communism is basic to living in society. It is presumptively eternal, a permanent sense of being mutually indebted. Exchange or reciprocity strives to achieve equivalence, so that indebtedness is temporary and should ideally be cancelled. Hierarchy is a permanent relationship between unequal parties. The rhetoric of reciprocity disguises the working principle, which is precedent. Debt here is irrevocable and transfers pass only one way (2014: 65).

Also permitting critical questioning of generosity as straightforward, unentailed giving was the existence in our data of a set of rules governing participation in "enabling" mentoring programs. Analysis of these rules provoked a question: if generosity was so defining of mentoring relationships, why did mentees need to take such great care in asking for and acquiring it? We argue that the carefully put requests for mentors to give (time, energy, resources, networks) to mentees indicates that generosity was anything but free flowing. Rather, it was situated as a limited good to be bestowed by those in positions to give on those in a position to receive. The clear result of our exploration of generosity in these ways is our claim that hierarchical relations characterise mentoring.

We are also interested in what Maussian insights about gift economies *cannot* reveal about giving and ostensible generosity. Here, inspired by Diprose's (2002) corporeal generosity, we contrast virtuous giving with a valuing of alterity. Applying this latter version of generosity to our data provides even further insight into how "enabling" mentoring programs array mentees and mentors in hierarchical relation. We conclude that, in terms of the subjugation of mentees to power, "enabling" versions of mentoring differ very little from the Homerian version so abhorred by critics, which demands the submission of the mentee to the conditions of patriarchal power.

We attend closely to the lively ways in which mentoring operates in the institutional world in practice, in a fine-grained analysis of the experiences of academic women located at all institutional levels, and in close analysis of the productions the university dispenses of mentoring—its texts, its vision statements, its core, and its stated values. At the first, this involves examining the patriarchy that mentoring programs seek to counter.

NOTES

1. Community Studies emerged principally from the Chicago School in the US and subsequently developed elsewhere, especially in the UK and (to a lesser extent) in Australia. Different national forms of interdisciplinary Community Studies emerged in Australia and Britain. Ostensibly, the two are differentiated by the dominance of Sociology and historically urban research in Australian Community Studies and the predominance of Anthropology and traditionally rural research in the British variant, but the most important and foundational difference lies precisely in how they each conceptualise conflict and community per se. These contexts share a substantive focus on the "village," a phenomenon that exists at different scales from the remote to the rural, suburban and urban, but is "rooted" fundamentally in relationships between people in close-knit social networks within and beyond the physicality of a place. There is a strong Community Studies tradition of incorporating multisitedness which recognises that villages increasingly extend beyond their obvious geographical boundaries. The conceptual development of "glocality" has seen analysis of community relations as they are practiced on social media platforms just as much as they are investigated between neighbours dwelling in a locale. Methodologically, predominantly ethnographic methods are deployed, and Community Studies in both contexts is dominated by Anthropology and Sociology. Conflict has never reached

conceptual maturity in Australian Community Studies because analysis of it is typically restricted to tensions between particular marginalised communities and the mainstream "community" from which they differ. Ethnic marginalisation and conflict that arises with the wider (white) Australian mainstream dominates the Australian Community Studies scholarly record (Noble & Poynting, 2010). In contrast, British Community Studies has retained this focus on local community with the result that a very broad range of communities, and all members of a community, are represented in Community Studies scholarship.

2. The authors are indebted to Professor Andrew Dawson for sharing his extensive knowledge of this history.

3. In a much more sinister vein, Wilson and Elman also note: "Data on this network runs in both directions. While the messages that mentors pass down will shape the future, the messages they send up can be vitally important also. This suggests another contribution of mentoring, the placement of 'deep sensors' within the organization. Mentors in their occasional role as deep sensors of workforce mood, attitude, etc., can transfer early warning signals to upper management long before news of such trouble becomes common knowledge, is communicated through formal channels, or manifests itself through reduced levels of performance. In discussing this deep sensing role, we are not suggesting that mentors should pass on specific information provided to them in confidence. Rather, we are suggesting that mentors are in a position to detect increasing levels of 'noise' emanating from various quarters within the organization before it becomes figural or specific information" (1990: 89).

Chapter 2

Know Imitate Thine Enemy

ATHENA'S ORIENTATION

In this chapter, we are not dealing with mentoring activity that is named as such. Beyond the parameters of a named program, advisements on how women can act to succeed in the institution are yet made, along with the identification of impediments to their institutional rise. Homer's Mentor is not in evidence, but Athena appears in one of her guises to provide counsel. In this chapter, we document her presence in the form of women-only promotion advisement sessions and in the processes of corporeal accounting that are intended to support female ascension.

In this chapter, we make a sustained examination and detailed analysis of that which mentoring ostensibly seeks to overthrow, or at least approach with key correctives: the patriarchy. We indulgently depend on a weaving analogy: besides being the goddess of wisdom and war, Athena was also the goddess of weaving. Male dominance is woven into the fabric of the institution. We could say that the longitudinal warp-threads of the institutional tapestry are held stationary by long male-dominated history, but a transverse female weft is drawn through it—this thread might be described as attempts at gender equity in patriarchal context. The pattern might change, but the structuring threads remain in place. This kind of analogy captures aptly how many feminist analysts describe the gains and the frustrations attached to chasing gender equity goals: the change in the pattern is slow to emerge, and what is achieved has to be accommodated by existing structural forms. But we take issue with the idea that the weft is fundamentally oriented in a different direction than is the warp thread. We actually think that warps and wefts are more accurately imagined as intimately entwined and supportive of one another. Accordingly, we raise the possibility in this chapter that mentoring is intimately involved in the reproduction of patriarchal patterns that makes powerful men—and, we argue—honorary men when it makes successful women. In this chapter, we examine how mentoring's structure mimics the structure of the patriarchy that it seeks to disrupt.

We begin this chapter with a potted history of the rise of the university in Australia, to orient the reader to the main events that have given rise to the university as we know it today. For a much more fulsome, throughgoing and comprehensive history of the modern Australian university, consult Forsyth, 2014. Imitation looms (!) large in our analysis. We follow that brief charting with a closer, ethnographically informed analysis of the effects of these events on gendered participation in the university; in other words, we examine the patriarchal conditions that women must contend with as a result of the rise of the neoliberal university. Here, we focus first on leadership and attempts underway at our own institution to support the promotion of women into leadership positions. We then turn to examine the corporeal accounting that women must do to explain and justify their departures from a male standard of academic performance. This requires biological and emotional labour—labour that goes not only unrecompensed but *unquestioned* as the male standard remains firmly in place. We examine these two examples in and through promotions advisements and corporeal accounting, noting with interest the role of imitation in success: it is, evidently, beneficial for women to mimic masculine performances in the neoliberal university, which itself came into existence through processes of imitation.

It is certainly worth noting that the early history of the institution is one of some imitation as Australia looked to Britain and America to model its own institutions. The University of Melbourne had established itself in the image of Harvard. The University of Iowa provided the blueprint for the University of Ballarat. In the intention for it to be a research university, The Australian National University mimicked John Hopkins, when it was established in 1946. In the newspapers of the day, it was declared "Australia's Oxford"; what Oxford and Cambridge were to Britain, what Harvard and Yale were to the US, ANU was to be to Australia.

For the ANU, the days of imitation are far from over. Now, the university casts its gaze once again to Harvard—or "Oxbridge"—depending on which public announcement about its comprehensive redesign one happens to catch. On 11 February 2020 in *The Australian* newspaper, reporter Jill Rowbotham's copy read,

> "The Australian National University must be the Oxbridge/Ivy League institution of the southern hemisphere but with an inclusive and distinctively Australian character," vice-chancellor Brian Schmidt has declared in an ambitious speech outlining his plans for the next five years.

In its October 30, 2013, edition, the student newspaper *Woroni* reported that (well prior to becoming vice chancellor) Schmidt had made the provocation that "the ANU must redesign itself as an elite, Harvard-style institution to differentiate it from other Australian universities." He made the remarks as part of his Order of Australia Association-ANU speech on Thursday 24 October, 2013, entitled "The future of the ANU and its role in Canberra." It was preceded by Schmidt's editorial of October 23, in which he remarked, "the winds are blowing the wrong way for ANU," with declining Federal Government research funding and indiscernible differentiation from other Australian universities—a radical departure from the ANU's founding story, as we describe it in what follows.

Certainly, before COVID-19, the ANU faced daunting challenges compared to the other Group of Eight universities. Its small student population (a function of its location in the sparsely populated capital city of Canberra)[1] practically rules out underwriting the costs of research by cross-subsidising them through undergraduate fees, as larger institutions in much more populous centres can. Under the current federal funding model, the dollar return to the institution per student is the same for all the universities—something Schmidt clearly regards as a very significant policy flaw. The ANU's especial standing as the national university brought into existence by legislation in the late 1940s, once saw it in receipt of funding separate from the other universities. But in 2002 it, too, was forced to shift into a competitive grants system, which has eroded its core funding block. Unable to effectively grow its student participation rate in the small inland city in which it is located the ANU must, Schmidt proposed in his Order of Australia speech, change its business model. In stark contrast with the other growing universities, ANU intended capping its participation rate at 20,000 students, making it comparable to the world's exclusive institutions: Oxford, Cambridge, Harvard, Yale, Princeton, Stanford. Since becoming the university's vice chancellor (in 2016), Schmidt worked towards making the university anew in those terms. Imitation was clearly still the name of the game for ANU as it sought to reinvent itself in the difficult circumstances of its location. COVID-19 has altered that course, bringing about a reduction in student numbers by quite other means; plans aside from recovery are presently on ice.

A different kind of imitation was undertaken by Australian universities in the 1980s, when comprehensive reforms to the public service were ushered in under the Hawke government. Universities have since imitated the government management forms to which they themselves were subject, drawing their members into processes of performance accountability, especially in the production of research as the university entered the knowledge economy. As Simon Marginson and Mark Considine (2000) note, imitation played a crucial role in the development of the form of the university as we presently know it. In the 1980s,

> A new instrumentalism began to pervade policy debates and its weapon of choice was the performance target. Senior management inside the university soon began to resent Canberra's string-pulling but found themselves powerless to resist these pressures. Canberra showed it could break from its prolix past and made its dependents do "more with less." Within two years the universities were found doing to their own faculties and schools what Canberra had just done to them. Budget siphoning, productivity cuts and strategic planning taxes soon pulled local authority into line with executive intentions . . . managerial imitation [w]as the most potent form of organisational learning available to universities. Imitation gave them a means both to meet external objectives and a way to fashion tools for reforming their own institutions. In this sense nothing proved to be more welcome than a tyrant at the door (32).

Doing "more with less" has once again emerged as an effective tool of rationalization. The tyrant at the door is ostensibly COVID-19, but the university sector in Australia is not able to turn to the government for rescue, which has been firmly situated as the real tyrant. Left out of the recent federal budget, excluded from employment rescue packages like Job Keeper, and reminded that they are still able to turn a profit from domestic student income, universities have not been supported in any obvious way by the State. This is perhaps most obvious in media coverage of the situation. In late May 2021, on the Australian Broadcasting Corporation (ABC)'s highly respected 7:30 Report current affairs program, the federal education minister, Alan Tudge, remarked that Australia's borders would remain closed to international arrivals until mid-2022 (Tudge, 2021). He said that, for international university students, Australia was worth waiting for—and recommended they pause their study plans until Australia reopened. Schmidt, appearing on the same program, hit back: "we'll be insolvent if I carry the can for the Government" (Schmidt, 2021)—a remark that also references the fact that ANU is the worst-affected university in terms of financial losses. In the midst of his emergency plans to bring chartered flights of students into Australia before all market share is lost to its European and American competitors, a much resented managerial imitation emerges as ANU staff have little choice but to do more with less. Their own, and the institution's futures, depend on it. ANU has to maintain the high international rankings that the institution needs to remain competitive in the international higher education market. That means being creative and innovative, upping the quality and using the conditions COVID-19 has visited upon the university to be creative and innovative. This is language that Simone has herself used to get her own school staff to abandon the expensive lecture (or lab) and tutorial model that can no longer be funded in favour of installing teaching modes that excite students and do not occupy as much of any academic's time. However improved, innovative and time efficient they are, they likely would not have occurred unless in response to the state pressure that has forced universities to once again apply the government's own version of efficiency. Where it refuses to prop up universities, universities refuse to prop up programs and areas that are a drag on its finances and future, or any people who do not measure up to its research performance standards. By doing nothing at all, the government forces institutions to reacquaint themselves with the tools they first took up in the 1980s. For some, the organisational imitation that has produced a much refashioned university has been truly lamentable, taking the institution away from its traditional pursuit of reason as an end in itself, and thoroughly entailing it in a research market. As Carmody (2013: 1) notes, the embeddedness of the university in the Enlightenment context that gave rise to it has always had the effect of positioning the university beyond or external to the world in which it is located. There, it occupied an especial place as a public institution, providing a home for debating of the very conditions of our governance (see for example Habermas, 1989). Now, so the lamentation goes, the university is thoroughly enmeshed in them.

A BRIEF HISTORY OF THE RISE OF THE UNIVERSITY

In what follows, we contextualise the emergence of the neoliberal university with information that services our arguments about the ways in which women's labour in particular is institutionally recognised and leveraged. We rely for the most part on Marginson and Considine's (2000) comprehensive work on the rise of the "enterprise" university; the interested reader should consult their work for a more detailed account.

The rise of the university in Australia began with the establishment of the University of Sydney in 1850. It was quickly followed, in 1853, by the University of Melbourne. In 1874, the University of Adelaide was established and then, in 1890, the University of Tasmania. By Federation in 1901 when Australia's population was just shy of 4 million there were fewer than 3,000 university students. These initial institutions were joined by the University of Queensland in 1909 and the University of Western Australia in 1911. The universities were controlled by their respective State governments and, by the middle of the second decade of the 1900s, were attended by just 0.1 percent of the Australian population. They were, profoundly, the preserve of a small, male student population.

To represent the interests of these six foundational universities, the Australian Vice Chancellors' Committee was formed in 1920. During the ensuing decade, the state-based universities operated alongside a range of "post-school" establishments—art schools, technical colleges, teacher-training institutes and other advanced education organisations (see Davis, 2012, for a full discussion). These "other" institutions originally issued only trade and/or technical certificates, diplomas and professional bachelor's degrees. Universities were differentiated from the technical colleges and the like by their participation in research. But research was by no means the main activity of these early Australian universities. That role was taken up by the Commonwealth Scientific and Industrial Research Organisation (CSIRO), established by the Australian government in 1926.[2]

By the beginning of WWII, Australia's population had reached seven million. Its institutions served 14,236 students, 10,354 of whom were degree students (81 were higher degree students). But a transformation of Australia's universities was about to begin. To regulate university enrolments, the Universities Commission was created and the Commonwealth Reconstruction Training Scheme (CRTS) was implemented, in 1942. As Marginson and Considine (2000) note, however, university growth remained slow until the end of the war, when the Federal Government found its coffers full—a result of winning its tussle with the states over income tax receipts. Higher education began to figure importantly in national economic growth. There was a huge increase in demand for teachers who could teach the baby boomer generation. The vision was very much of the elite, small university system that could produce paraprofessional and technical training for the growing Australian workforce. As a result of the CRTS, by 1948 there were 32,000 students enrolled—an effective doubling of the 1941 participation rate. By 1949, another university—the University of New South Wales (UNSW)—had come into existence as, principally, a teaching university.

The arrival of UNSW had been preceded, in 1946, by the establishment of the Australian National University which was created by an Act of Federal Parliament as a national research-only institution; that is, it was dedicated to research and postgraduate research training for national purposes. Its mandate stood in contrast to the pursuit of national interests made in the terms of economic and technical gains to shore up the Australian postwar economy in which the other universities were chiefly involved. People would have to learn new skills in a postwar economy; universities could be used as a national resource—as exploitable as any other. But the national university would make its contribution in and through research. In Curtin's government, Minister for Post War Reconstruction John Dedman proclaimed the university would lead the way in translating for civilian use the gains that had been made in medicine during the war (the purview of the John Curtin School of Medical Research); it would also secure the benefits from developments in scientific and human relations and operate as a major player in Pacific affairs. Presently, the university continues to deliver on those fronts, framing its importance around prosecuting its unique national responsibilities. In his 2019 State of the University address, for example, the Chancellor, Gareth Evans, did what his predecessors had done, reporting on ANU's contributions to national policy debates around geopolitics and economics of the Asia Pacific region, the annual hosting of a forum of leaders from the public, business, community, and academic sectors to debate "the great political, economic and social policy issues of the day, and consolidating the Forum's reputation as Australia's Davos" (Evans, 2019).

After the establishment of ANU, the Menzies government dramatically extended federal involvement in the higher education sector begun at the end of the war. It introduced the Commonwealth scholarship scheme in 1951, to cover student fees. It paid a means-tested allowance for talented students from lower socioeconomic groups. The State Grants (Universities) Act of 1951 saw the Commonwealth contribute one quarter of the recurrent costs of state universities, a result of the Mills Committee Inquiry into university finances. In 1954, the same year that the University of New England was established, Prime Minister Robert Menzies established the Committee on Australian Universities. The Murray Committee Inquiry (in 1957), which found that financial stringency was responsible for the overall poor performances of institutions, led to increased funding to the sector from the Commonwealth Government. Menzies's government tripled federal government funding. This resulted in very significant increases in academic salaries, investment in built institutional environments, and the establishment of a permanent committee to oversee and make recommendations concerning higher education. By the end of the 1950s, female enrolments began to increase, and their portion of total enrolments has steadily increased since that time.

Just as the Murray Report had situated universities in a utilitarian imaginary, seeing them as instruments to work national public policy objectives through academic purposes, the Martin Report of 1964 saw higher education as enabling self-development. Marginson and Considine note that Martin argued,

> the private gains to be achieved by students were "only a fraction" of what society itself would achieve as more and more people became educated. This was not the "civilising" project which had once brought reformers into the debate about primary and secondary schooling. Rather it showed how far the Keynesian logic of consensus had stretched into all fields of public policy (2000: 35).

The desire to link educational objectives to the national economic interest would result in a complete transformation of higher education from a semi-private domain of upper class culture and state-based training for the elite professions "into a system of mass credentialing designed to capture the spirit of optimism of the long boom" (Marginson & Considine, 2000: 34). At this time, the postwar baby boom exerted enormous pressure to increase the number of universities. It led to the establishment of the universities known as the "Gumtree" universities—Griffith, Macquarie, La Trobe, Flinders, Murdoch and Newcastle.

By 1973, the Commonwealth had full control over universities. In that year, the Whitlam government abolished fees and assumed full financial responsibility for them. The establishment of James Cook University (1970), Griffith University (1971), Deakin University (1974), Murdoch University (1975), and the University of Wollongong (1975) meant that by 1975 there were 148,000 students enrolled in 19 universities. Whitlam's ambitions were to achieve greater equity in higher education, and to make it available to a much broader diversity of students.

The Keynesian principles of manipulating demand and supply that were to come into their own in the form of the Public Management model (which emerged fulsomely during the 1980s) did not go so far as to intervene when, as was the case under Whitlam, the levers did not produce the desired results: it was clear that the main beneficiaries of the expansion of enrolments and universities continued to be wealthy middle-class students. We have heard some in the university community wonder whether or not this outcome has reached its full capacity to harm the institution. One senior professor from a Go8 university remarked in an acid tone how universities—especially those with a stated intention to become elite—had failed to diversify along the lines that earlier massification had made possible. Not only that, he felt; they would fare very badly in a COVID-19 world where universities turned to the publics they had abandoned to "donate them out of trouble." Indeed, so far, philanthropic saviours have failed to appear.

Women did appear to benefit significantly, however. Denise Bradley (former vice chancellor and president of the University of South Australia and leader of the 2008 Bradley Review of Higher Education) recalled of the period on the Australian Broadcasting Corporation (ABC)'s Radio National program:

> The universities that really profited from that were the universities which I call the gumtree universities, which were more flexible, which were under more pressure for students, and which moved very, very rapidly to provide all kinds of programs and things like childcare for women. And of course what they got largely was an extraordinarily focused and committed group of intelligent women who'd been in the past discriminated against in their access to university (ABC Radio National, 02 July 2013).

As we will suggest later in this chapter, the "past" of discrimination is not over; gendered discrimination remains in institutions in a range of ways.

The free education offered under the Whitlam government ended with the 1983 election of the Hawke government. Culminating in the late 1980s and early 1990s, the higher education sector was, profoundly, managerialised (see Blackmore & Sachs, 2007), marking a new phase of its existence.

The school retention rate had increased immensely during the 1980s, and the university system as it stood was not equipped to accommodate these extra students. The labour market was changing; there was an increased requirement for professional skills. The new government had to solve these problems. When it came to power, Australia had three distinctly different higher education sectors: institutes, colleges and universities. Each granted degrees and claimed a research tradition. Although it was technically tripartite, in essence this system was binary, with the proper universities on one side, the technical colleges and institutes on the other. Hawke's Education and Training Minster John Dawkins set out with an ambitious and rapid plan for change. He ushered in the Unified National System (UNS). He required the colleges of advanced education and institutes of technology to either merge with existing universities or to themselves become universities. Each of the thirty-six universities that emerged at the end of the process (seventeen more than had existed prior to the reforms) had to be committed to *research*, to professional programs, and to the titles, nomenclature and operating procedures of the nation's founding institutions. More competitive relationships emerged between individual institutions as a result; the uniqueness claimed by each institution was cloaked by the required universality of the UNS. In the context of COVID-19, one might expect that fewer universities (or parts of universities—faculties, departments) would emerge than presently populate the sector in, perhaps, another imitation of the history of rationalisation. As that history has shown, politics are inextricably intertwined with universities. When Dawkins oversaw the last major contraction of institutions, the politics were about research, about massification, about standardisation, and funding. Market forces and budgetary contractions will be part of the story once again and we will soon see if the government regards leaving all players in play politically expedient.

Dawkins decreed there would be financial support for institutions with a minimum of 2,000 full-time students. He reintroduced student fees, but he did so in an innovative way: via an income-contingent loan system that meant free entry and repayment of a fixed amount after earnings exceed a certain threshold (a scheme known as the Higher Education Contribution Scheme, HECS). The reinvestment of those fees into the system created new places, resulting in a massive expansion in student enrolments. Not only were students required to make a co-payment for education services; universities were also encouraged to find other, full fee paying, students: international students. This would permit governments to further reduce financial commitment to universities, which increasingly exposed themselves to international markets (see for example Harvey & Newton, 2004; Deem et al., 2008; Morley, 2003, 2014; Lafferty & Fleming, 2000).[3] The reversal of fortunes caused by the COVID-19 pandemic provides an index of just how much universities did so.

The changes were difficult; merging institutions meant merging cultures; the most difficult were mergers between institutions that had histories of research activity and those that did not. Peter Noonan, former adviser to Dawkins, recalled on ABC Radio National in 2013 that "people were suddenly perceived to be not performing because they weren't producing research" (Phillips, 2013). Indeed, the requirement for research to be fundamental to the mission of a university had the dramatic effect of narrowing the academic basis, in specific respect of the devaluing of teaching. As Glyn Davis notes, "Teaching staff lost out to those who combine teaching with research. A 1965 survey found that around 21 per cent of academic staff in Australia were focused principally on teaching. By the 1990s this number had declined to just 3.5 per cent" (2012: 34).

The 1980s saw a more management-centred approach come into vogue, with much more power given to leadership—whose chief purpose appeared to be to extract more information from subordinates with which to measure their performance. Efficiency imperatives worked their way into everyday government operations, and they worked their way into universities, giving rise to entrepreneurial management systems. They self-regulated, using the targets, management plans and performance controls with which members are so deeply familiar today. Marginson and Considine note of the period:

> The Green Paper, Higher education: a policy discussion paper (1987), released shortly after his [Dawkins's] ascent to power, was as bold and threatening a document as the universities had ever faced. . . . It lampooned university management practices as inefficient and in particular made fun of the academy's collegial practices such as electing deans. Closely linked to these structural changes the report championed the idea that higher education be viewed as an industry. Dawkins and his supporters also saw great opportunity for this "education industry" to export its product into Asia, thus helping improve the current account deficit which was so much on the mind of the Government at this time (2000: 43).

The wholesale adoption of the changes demanded by Dawkins, within only a few years of their announcement, emerged in:

> the new and more mobile forms of executive power, the growth of Deputy Vice-Chancellor (DVC) and Pro Vice-Chancellor (PVC) positions and executive

Deans, the Vice-Chancellor's executive groups at the operational hub of the universities, the role of budget systems and "drivers," the declining role of Academic Boards and changing character of Councils, [and] the running of research as a system of measured performance (2000: 21).[4]

Public universities were not the first targets of the neoliberal turn of the 1980s. The privatisation of public goods and the wholesale restructure of the economy around competition was priorly applied to utilities and public transport—and the principles were applied to the public service, which found itself subject to accountability principles, target achievement and intensive managerialism. For universities the process has been an incremental one, involving the increasing application of business practices to them as if they were for-profit corporations.

While the changes resulted in the shifting of a very significant proportion of the financial responsibility for higher education, universities are not by any means the same as for-profit corporations. They exist somewhere in between public institution and for-profit business. Much of the authorship of their lives lies beyond them, remaining in the hands of government. Decisions pertaining to capping student numbers or fee deregulation, for instance, are government decisions.

At no time has this been more evident than during the financial crisis experienced by universities as a result of COVID-19. The Australian Prime Minister, Scott Morrison, has consistently declared universities firmly within the category of for-profit corporations—to date, this has been consequential with respect to securing government assistance for the sector as it flails as a result of its exposure to the full-fee-paying international student market. That investment has been so strong that in 2017, when he was Treasurer, Morrison applied a 2.5 percent efficiency dividend to the sector. But at the time of their introduction, a good deal of artfulness was needed to apply neoliberal policies to universities. Essentially, a blend of free market rhetoric and intense bureaucratic control brought them around (see Lorenz, 2012). Now, in the midst of the COVID-19 crisis, the extent of the institutional embrace of the market has become extremely problematic. As Ng (2020) says, education is now Australia's third-largest export, surpassed only by exports of iron ore and coal. In 2018/19 alone, it contributed $37.6 billion to the Australian economy. That stunning figure has, of course, been enabled by the corporatisation of the university structure we have just described. Universities have been increasingly pushed to participate in corporate activity so as to become less reliant on a shrinking government contribution. The international student market presented a solution, and it was rapidly exploited. As Ng (2020) notes, the new wealth delivered into the university system (as well as into the economy more generally) saw significant upticks in executive salaries, making universities look very much like corporate entities. But, universities are non-profit entities and therefore really cannot function as corporations do.

One of the things they cannot do very effectively is convert surpluses into assets. The built environs are certainly worth a considerable amount—but they do not themselves generate funding. As Ng points out, the people—who conduct specialist original research, and impart knowledge—are the real assets—but

> academics are converted into liabilities in the form of salaries that must be paid, while the students are translated into a revenue stream that must be ever-increased, even though the university has no ability to capture profits for the longer term. As non-profit entities, universities must ensure that any prof-its are expended by the end of the financial year. The surpluses they have run for decades have therefore disappeared and were always going to disappear. Corporatisation has promoted greater efficiencies and the continual increase of profit, but also incentivised universities to increase expenditure. . . . The justi-fication for these expenses has been that universities need improved facilities to attract more international students, because international students are needed to fund universities. COVID-19 has now exposed the tautological nature of this argument. It is evident that increasing the numbers of international students in the system has not helped the university achieve financial independence. They have instead simply made the university more dependent on funding from inter-national students. Now that this revenue stream has dried up, the universities' inability to make use of its surplus capital has become apparent (Ng, 2020: np).

If the reforms narrowed the academic and financial bases of the university, then they equally narrowed the distance implied in mythologies between the university and the social. Instead of standing at some distance from the society it framed and interpreted, it now stands in direct competition with a society made over in its image: "a technologically enhanced knowledge-driven form of the social whose commitment to ceaseless innovation and commodity cre-ation leaves the university little ground on which to stand apart, or to defend more traditional values." As Roberts (1999) notes, the social acceptance of the "market metanarrative" is such that liberal democracies are no longer prepared to sustain public goods (or public universities). Instead, the task of the state—at least since the Hawke and Keating years—has been to create and sustain an institutional scaffold that facilitates market rationality—despite the ostensible preference for deregulation (see Harvey, 2005: 3). The public and critical role of the university is resultantly undermined as "knowledge" itself became, increasingly, a valuable commodity, yielding the "knowledge economy" (Davis, 2012: 35).

Knowledge itself was the key to the relevance of universities to a new economy: it could generate a product of worth within an international system.

What counts in the knowledge economy limits the range of and possibilities for research, and for its value; thus, the production of research is enclosed within value parameters that serve to classify it in accordance with its worth to the economy. As Blackmore notes, "the doxa of higher education as a public good has been unsettled as universities are no longer the only source or producers of knowledge legitimating what counts as valued knowledge" (2015: 180).

New technologies and mobile students and academics have facilitated the globalisation of this academic capitalism, intensifying it (Slaughter & Leslie, 1997; Blackmore & Sachs, 2007; Marginson & Considine, 2000). Blackmore says of it:

> This resulted in a blurring of public/private provision, a renewed focus on branding and ranking, moves towards institutional restructuring to encourage interdisciplinarity, demand-driven online curriculum, industry partnerships and the intensification of academic work (Blackmore, 2015: 180; see also Epstein, Boden, Deem, Rizvi & Wright, 2008; and Menzies & Newson, 2008).

The rise of a worldwide pandemic has, of course, laid waste—at least for the time being—to the investment that universities have made in overseas markets. How universities will rebuild participation is not yet clear beyond emergency flights bringing small numbers of international students in, and keeping up excellence indicators—especially since, as noted, government assistance has not been forthcoming in Australia. The language from the sector is becoming increasingly alarmed—as Schmidt's afore-cited remarks to the ABC's 7:30 Report indicate—but the squeeze on the sector began much earlier. Opportunity to reorient university business toward a devastated economy was taken in June 2020, when the then education minister, Dan Tehan, revealed an overhaul of tertiary education. The plan favoured "job relevant" courses, whose fees are set to be dramatically reduced. Humanities course fees are set to double. The plan includes an extra 39,000 university places for Australian students that will be funded by 2023.

ABC News reported on 19 June 2020 that the announcement came in a context of doubled enrolment application figures for 2021, in part a result of travel restrictions that mean students can no longer take a gap year between secondary and tertiary study. Typically, about 20,000 high school seniors defer university entry in favour of travel, or to take up "gap" employment. The latter option is unavailable owing to a serious downturn in the employment market; under those circumstances, university applications typically rise. The turn from humanities and toward STEMM disciplines is designed to funnel students into the industries the government believes will drive future job growth. Unsurprisingly, the plan drew sharp criticism from universities that have long decried the business-oriented focus of universities, but it is by absolutely no means a new or surprising development (see Duffy, 2020).

Participation in the knowledge economy has required a new performance of academics and new quality assurance measures to assess and indeed beget it (see Cooper, 2007). The financial control retained by government permits it extensive control over the sector in and through the creation and application of quality assurance measures. Measurements of research output, the most highly valued commodity on the international higher education market, are implemented to assess productivity and performance (Deem, Hillyard & Reem, 2008; Grummell, Devine & Lynch, 2009), thus fundamentally,

> altering the ways in which research "quality" is measured and subsequently valued by those inside and outside of the academy. Moreover, quality of research becomes not just a matter of whether academics publish their research, but about what they publish, where they publish it, and how often it is cited (Lipton, 2015: 62).

These conditions have resulted in change to academic habitus, as Blackmore notes:

> Within global higher education markets, research remains critical to the distinctiveness of both the field and the status of an individual university and its positioning relative to the state and other educational providers . . . the research activities of academics [can be thought of, in Bourdieusian terms] as scientific (research) capital that includes symbolic capital in terms of esteem, international networks and material capital or findings (Blackmore, 2015: 180; see also Bourdieu, 1988).

In 2013, Randell-Moon, Saltmarsh and Sutherland-Smith described this new habitus. They reported the findings of their 2010 examination of academics' relationships to this relatively new definition of research. Drawn from data collected across 16 institutions, the main finding was that participants felt they could not think freely, did not have control over their own research agendas and were subject to the contagion of the managerial and audit culture ushered in with neoliberalism. The authors note that,

> neoliberal reforms to the academy have created a research culture that treats academics as non-thinking entities (the living dead), who feel they have limited control over their research and funding amidst a pervasive and contagious audit culture (2013: 57).

They also note that,

whilst these reforms may be experienced by academics as an externally introduced form of control that saps or sucks the "life" out of research activity, the
proliferation of neoliberal reforms is only enabled through the complicit reproduction of an audit culture by academics themselves. In this sense, academics
(as the dead living) also contribute, in ambivalent and contradictory ways, to the
zombification of the academy (2013: 58).

This is something from which the authors implore academics to immediately
and aggressively *desist* so that they can begin to *resist.* The plea is made
on the grounds that a key mythology—the pleasures of being a free thinker
who can indulge in the passions of the mind. This mythology does not abate
under conditions of neoliberalism; instead it produces what Berlant (2011)
describes as "cruel optimism"; researchers continue to dedicate themselves
to research but cannot challenge the conditions under which it occurs. They
must endure increasing administrative work that services counting and clas-
sifying, such is the extent of their commitment, leading Gill (2010) to dub
them ideal neoliberal subjects. Others have remarked similarly, noting that
academic life is marked by ambivalence, contradiction and paradox (see
Blackmore & Sachs, 2007). The self-managing academic both opposes and
accommodates the corporatisation of their everyday practice as they struggle
between the dulling effects of compliance regimes and their desire to excel,
being both competitive and collegial (Bansel & Davies, 2010). At the same
time, they are sidelined as decision-makers, experts and creative agents
within their own institutions (Boden & Epstein, 2006).

As Cooper (2007) notes, the university was caught between its traditional
role as a public-oriented institution with the means to critically reflect and
interpret society on the one hand, and its emerging role as a generator of
knowledge for the high-tech economy on the other. The contradiction was
managed (or perhaps reconciled) with the benefits of increased numbers of
students, and the apparent overthrow of the elite nature of university education. Cooper (2007) puts the absence of any "research war" or "knowledge
war" or "education war" against these changes, predicted to be fought with
all the veracity of the culture wars, down to precisely these beneficial fac-
tors—or, at least, they are very beneficial to some. Cooper goes so far as to
say that the Dawkins reforms resulted in academic Darwinism, privileging
the labour of those whose work could readily acquire value in the knowledge economy (like economics or law) over those whose work could not
(like the visual arts, music). But perhaps it was not as straightforward as all
that. Neoliberalism has been able to assert itself as the common-sense view
of the world (Harvey, 2005: 3), and has not, therefore, brooked the kind of
resistance it otherwise might. As Shore and McLauchlan (2012) show in their
ethnographic study of academics, profit arising from private investment and

knowledge transfer has come to signify public good in relation to knowledge production within the university community itself. This changed discourse is responsible for the lack of outcry: commodification has been wholly normalised. This is easy enough to appreciate in everyday conversations at the university; we express the ideology of the market turn every day of the week in ordinary conversations about how to pitch this or that idea so that it generates money and so that it is of appreciable public worth. As Strachan et al. (2016) demonstrate, those kinds of conversations might well be dominated by male academics. Women academics are far less likely to attract industry funding, and are far less likely to be working in the national research priority areas defined by the government and reflected in the funding rules and conditions of the Australian Research Council (ARC) or the National Health and Medical Research Council (NHMRC), Australia's chief academic research funding bodies. It is also easy enough to appreciate that such systems harbour a decided preference for innovators, and especially for "scientists, technicians and business-people [dominated by men] rather than social scientists or those trained in the humanities [dominated by women]" (Shore & McLauchlan, 2012: 281; see also Ahmed, 2006; Feteris, 2012; Fitzgerald & Wilkinson, 2010; Probert, 2005; White, Carvalho & Riordan, 2011).

Dominant research methods are those where "rigour" is pursued "with a certain scientific rationality—one that valorises precision, systematicity, objectivity and the advancement of knowledge" (Clark, Floyd & Wright, 2006, quoted in Phillips, 2014: 316). Rigour is that which is hard, strict, and severe, and is understood as essential to research practice. Rigorous work *measures* (Phillips, 2014; see also Lipton, 2020: 23). The masculine legacy of science, as a privileged mode of inquiry replete with the qualities of rigour, rationality, systematicity, objectivity, and measurement, rises to prominence in neoliberal regimes. While humanities and social sciences remain strongly present in the academy, they have had to ensure their relevance. Theoretical knowledge—knowledge for knowledge's sake—has no place in a labour market where applied knowledge and skills matter most.

Women academics tend to work in fields that are less likely to attract industry funding (Strachan et al., 2016), and are less likely to be considered as working in national research priority areas. These all influence women's academic membership and career progression (Ahmed, 2006; Feteris, 2012; Fitzgerald & Wilkinson, 2010; Probert, 2005; White, Carvalho & Riordan, 2011). This is something with which Simone has taken particular issue; one of the effects of neoliberalism on researching human social life has been to press findings into the service of solving problems for identifiable end users. As Simone has found in her own research on licit drug use, pressing research inquiries and findings into the service of problem alleviation tends to enclose research enquiries to that which is useful, relevant and impactful, with the result that only certain kinds of research inquiries can be raised and addressed (see Dennis, 2016). As Thornton writes,

> "skills" have supplanted traditional forms of knowledge in the public imagination as to what is deemed to be most desirable in a university education, as they have come to be associated with modernisation, success and productivity. . . . Universities are therefore expected to demonstrate their "usefulness" by training large numbers of productive workers to support the new knowledge economy and by generating academic capitalism through research (Thornton, 2015: 3).

Ferree and Zippel (2015) argue that academic capitalism is set against the classic liberal university and that the latter is imagined in highly romantic terms. These terms, they argue, forget the exclusion of women (and less privileged men) from the liberal university, the colonial expansion of higher education in the service of empire,

> and the unacknowledged positionality that infuses standards of only supposedly value-free science. Hard struggles over the boundaries of political liberalism in the late twentieth century were necessary to expand notions of citizenship, equal treatment, self-governance, and human rights to parts of the human race—especially but not exclusively female-bodied people—previously excluded in whole or in part from these norms (2015: 565).

These battles are not won in the twenty-first century.

FEMALE PARTICIPATION IN THE NEOLIBERAL INSTITUTION

The gendered paradox of academic promotion is closely tied to measures and values. The paradox is that the more emphasis that is placed on the presence and achievements of women, the less critical attention is paid to women's experiences of discrimination and marginalisation that endure in light of their prominence. Academic women's participation and performativity in the contemporary university is situated within a social, political and economic climate of metrics and valuation. A misunderstanding or misrecognition of women's contributions is a value problem. Women's value to the academic enterprise is not properly seen and understood by those in senior leadership and decision-making roles. Measurement is used selectively in relation to gender. It is ignored, as Morley (2011) observes, when women suffer discrimination and underrepresentation and yet it is intensified when women overrepresent and pose a threat to a dominant group or workplace culture. Morley (2011) describes this as "misogyny posing as measurement."

In the thick of the neoliberal shift toward the corporatisation and privatisation of the public sector—including universities—legislation was introduced to deal with gender inequity. Instruments included the *Federal Affirmative Action Act 1986*, and the *Equal Employment Opportunity for Women in the Workplace Act 1999*. Under the latter, as Bacchi (2000) notes, employers could take "reasonably practicable actions" with an emphasis on government facilitation rather than disciplinary or castigatory action in response to any noncompliance. Those terms—"reasonable" and "practicable"—signal for Bacchi that institutions take less seriously their obligations to see gender equity through (Bacchi, 2000: 68; see also Ahmed, 2006: 747, who argues that "equality fails because institutions have failed to take equality seriously."

Deem and Ozga (1997) argue that neoliberalism effectively converts equality into diversity (see also Skeggs, 2014). Here, difference and variety acquire worth because they articulate the individual accomplishments that are accorded high value in the neoliberal institution. As Marginson and Considine (2000: 9) note, the centralisation of hierarchical executive power brings about the decline and devaluing of collegial forms of governance that tend to undergird equity. According to Skeggs, our subjectivities adapt to fit these kinds of values and structures "to the extent that we become the living embodiment of capital" (2014: 2).

Ahmed (2012) argues that in respect to both diversity and equality, the existence of policy lends a security that is not borne out in substantive action or any kind of social or political transformation. Diversity is only acknowledgment of difference that confers positive feelings among institutional members, and equality can be presumed to be achieved "in the act" of legislating (Ahmed, 2012: 11). Diversity and equity policies, in other words, become substitutes for action. This observation is important; as Ahmed says it is in the shallow discourse of equity and diversity that women's marginalisation and underrepresentation are rendered invisible, and the professoriate, journal editorship roles and executive institutional roles remain dominated by men (Fotaki, 2013).

Ahmed's point is relevant, too, in the context of rising female participation in the academy. Although female participation in the institution *is* rising, numerical increases in the female labour force can easily obfuscate the effects of the neoliberal research enterprise. Drawing on sector-wide data supplied by the Australian Department of Education and Training for the period 2008–2017, Frank Larkins, former vice chancellor of the University of Melbourne, produced an LH Martin Institute report on the state of gendered play across the higher education sector in Australia (Larkins, 2018). The report indicates that universities have recruited more female staff (academic and nonacademic) than male staff over the past decade. Overall, it is a hefty number: from 2008–2017, 66 percent of all new hires were women. Resultantly, the proportion of female staff increased from 54.7 percent in 2008 to 57.0 percent in 2017. The net effect has been that the gender gap for academic staff has been reduced to around 5 percent (in favour of males). More full-time staff are female, with the proportion increasing over the decade from 50.3 percent to 52.6 percent, but fractional full-time staff statistics are dominated by females: almost 70 percent are female. An "historic landmark" is then declared by Larkins to have been achieved, "with more female university staff being tenured than males." Speaking generally of the sector, Larkins's analysis declares that "more females are now being appointed at the senior lecturer and above levels than at any previous time" (2018: 2).

Such declarations, however, obscure the low participation of women in the STEM disciplines that are of highest value to the knowledge economy. Data collected for the first time in the ERA 2015 and 2018 evaluation rounds in the service of the production of a report titled *Gender and the Research Workforce* (see Australian Research Council, 2018) provides gender participation rates by field of research. The picture is clear: women have far lower participation rates in the (STEM) disciplines of highest worth in the current context in which research is valued.

The report also indicates that there are more female researchers employed at Level B (52 percent) and those classified as nonacademic positions (60 percent) than there are males. For all other levels, particularly at higher academic levels, there is a much smaller percentage of females. For those universities that distinguish themselves as research institutions, numbers like these are telling, for research is the key valuable produced by the university, and success in this realm trumps success in others. Also telling is the fact that across the sector, women continue to dominate in nonacademic positions in universities and stands presently at 66 percent. Such figures indicate that it is deeply problematic to assume, as "pipeline" theory does, that a critical mass of women will be promoted into research leadership (see Bell, 2009).

Because equity has clearly not come to pass in the form of the equal participation of women across all levels of the university, institutions have typically implemented equity and diversity programs to equip women to navigate the terrain. The very fact that women have to be supplied with a roadmap to navigate the institutional landscape indicates its inhospitability, but as Feteris (2012) writes, the instructions for wayfinding are far worse: she notes that "the only path to success is for women to learn to become honorary men" (2012: np). Becoming an honorary man is a very particular form of imitation that we examine closely in the remainder of this chapter.

TO WALK LIKE A MAN: INSTITUTIONAL LEADERSHIP

Leadership came up in a very specific way during our fieldwork, and especialy for key informant Alison, in the context of a particular mentoring activity: preparing women for promotion. Here, she contemplated perhaps the starkest examples of the ways in which mentoring might function to effectively make men out of women as the latter seek to become "successful."

Women-only promotion advice sessions might be understood as a specific version of short-term mentoring. In them, successful academics give women who are contemplating promotion advice peculiar to the preparation of an application and the prosecution of a face-to-face interview.

In such sessions women who want to be promoted are provided with information that will make it more likely that they will be successful in their applications. These sessions make clear what is otherwise tacit and hidden: the secrets of male success, and exactly how to replicate them, right down to the physical bearing of "masculine confidence" that a woman could exude if she entered her promotion interview as a man would, rather than adopting the "passive" postures that the session leader said she had observed "too often" in women candidates.

In the sessions provided for women in preparation for their promotions, we sat with several dozen women as they took their seats in the closed-door session. A senior female member of the university rose from a low table at the front of the room when everyone was settled and introduced herself to the assembled group. She began the session by providing some context for running women-only sessions. They were, she said, offered in the context of "the patriarchy in which we live." It was important that women changed this, she suggested, by being promoted. To make her point, the session leader referenced a major ARC-funded study carried out in 2011; comparisons between the relative share of women and men across academic levels showed a male-dominated gender gap at the doctoral level which subsequently widened in increasing levels over an academic career. The data indicated that women were not only underrepresented in the professoriate. They were also grossly underrepresented in movements into the professoriate. To boot, predictions made in a Universities Australia study carried out in 2005 by Winchester and Browning painted a grim future picture (Winchester & Browning, 2005). The study investigated promotions policies and practices in thirty-four of Australia's thirty-nine universities to evaluate progress towards gender equity and the success rates of female applicants for promotion. The study was based on the commonly accepted assertions that women are less likely to apply for promotion, are more reticent in putting themselves forward, are less successful in applying for promotion than men, are more likely to experience career interruptions than men, and are overrepresented in the disciplines that do not attract large research grants (Winchester, Lorenzo, Browning & Chesterman, 2006: 506). The hypothesis was that academic promotion policies that do not take career interruptions into account and focus primarily on research as criteria would disadvantage women and constitute barriers to promotion. However, the study found that there was generally good practice right across the sector in relation to promotion policies and practices, and that there were good success rates for those women who did apply. In fact, women were more successful than men in promotions processes, a benefit of transparent policy. The analysis of the data found that, over time, the promotion barrier had shifted from Level C to Level D (senior lecturer to associate professor), but that it would take a full forty-nine years to achieve parity in the professoriate at the rate of progress at that time (Winchester, Chesterman, Lorenzo & Browning, 2005: 31). Who wanted to wait so long? Who could not see that it was not, in fact, flawed university policy—the problem came down to inadequate performances. This, said the session leader, *must* change.

Women, attendees were told, waited far longer than men to "go," even though they had "the goods." This made it difficult for the university to "see" them, hiding as they did behind a passivity of expression that belied their leadership and their autonomous labour. They were told, then, how to make that leadership and labour appear. Participants were told to talk like men.

The session leader informed the assembled women that, unlike women applying for promotion, men spoke in active terms. They appeared autonomous, their authority plainly in evidence. Participants were told that talking like a man involved, among other things, replacing the use of *we* with *I* in order to claim the valuable capital associated with making decisions and leadership. Turning passive descriptions of one's labour into active declarations of leadership could clearly distinguish "my" role from work accomplished in collectivity. Attendees were implored by the session leader to "use verbs to describe your work, like men do, instead of passive descriptions, like women tend to do." Wherever possible, women were specifically advised to abandon phrases like "I helped to achieve . . . " or "as a member of a team I . . . ," in favour of *"I led,"* or *"I achieved this."* We were advised that while our own institution was fully supportive of women, wanted to promote them and wanted to exhibit leadership in this space, promotion had been historically harder for women and there was "pressure to prove we're as good as men." Women were also advised to "command a room" in and through their posture. "Walk in with confidence. Sit confidently at the interview. Exude it."

This advice made Simone recall with great discomfort the occasion of her own professorial promotion interview. Nervous and wearing trousers that made her itchy but looked, in her own estimation, suitably serious, Simone attempted to enter the building in which the interview was to be held via the exit door. Realizing her error only after a member of the promotions panel saw her and pointed through the glass to the more conventionally used entry door, Simone recalled similar advice she'd been given about exuding confidence, as if the professorship was already hers. Squaring her shoulders resolutely, she entered her interview and declared to the promotions committee that it took a real leader to try new things, and not to follow others through the doors of conventional wisdom. Others with whom we spoke regarded the advice they were getting with great trepidation, especially as they felt they needed to prepare their bodies for reading as carefully as they'd prepared their applications, as we suggest was the case for Annabel, whose experience we describe below.

Replications of success could be borne in and through the female body in walk and talk, with the effect that the disadvantage attached to women's bodies could be reformulated, ironically, to an approximation of male performance. Similar advice had been given to some of our informants, who had been advised on completing their PhDs to "dress androgynously" and speak "clearly and slowly with total authority" when they were going for academic job interviews. This caused a great deal of stress to one informant, Annabel, who was just about to go for a job, felt more comfortable in dresses with her hair, nails and makeup done than she did in pants and a shirt. She worried about the way she talked ahead of her interview. She was bubbly and exuded a great deal of energy and enthusiasm when engaged on the topic of her research. On receiving her mentor's advisements, Annabel wondered,

> Will I be viewed as a little girl if I speak to quickly and excitedly about something I care deeply about? Especially if I am wearing a dress? This is not something I thought I would need to worry about. I spent all my time cranking out publications and teaching my ass off, not buying men's pants and seeing a voice coach. Have I really invested in the wrong things?

We note here that these orientations do not issue only from the workplace itself, nor do they necessarily come from encounters with men. In a now infamous Twitter case, Parinaz, a female PhD student, had been invited to give a talk at the University of Alberta. She was asked to supply a photo that could be circulated with her abstract, to advertise her upcoming talk. As Alberta is "cowboy country," she sent in a photo of her standing in front of a pickup truck on the main street of small town. She is pictured dressed in a lovely yellow long sleeve, high necked shirt, and jeans. Soon after Parinaz sent in the photo she was emailed by a female administrator. The email advised Parinaz that her photo was inappropriate, and that it had made female engineering students uncomfortable. Outrage ensued: Parinaz was inundated with messages of support. The question of whether such a thing had or would ever happen to a male PhD student was consistently raised. But the comments were not consistently outraged and supportive.

One female respondent remarked, "I don't think this pic is helping your career. It gives you short-term attention, but silently hurts your chances of building long-term professional relationships. Being attractive is unfortunately a double-edged sword for women." Another woman said, "The pic reminds me of a topless woman posing on a cool car. Like from a pin up calendar. Made for men. I know she is fully covered, but the association is there. I want to protect her [from people] seeing her like that."

In these remarks, complex relations with patriarchal forms and masculine dominance are in evidence. The remarks warn of its all-pervasive presence and attempt to advise in cautionary terms the implications of appearing in it as a woman in its own terms. "It is just my own experience and observation trying to understand why women are professionally discriminated against and what we can do to avoid falling into traps," wrote one concerned woman. "Yes, unfortunately we are judged based on our appearance." These tweets hit home for Alison who, in the early stages of her very first continuing academic post had been told by a female colleague, "it would have been easier for you to get your job because of the way you look."

It hit home more recently for Simone, who grew her hair out that she'd always kept short and seriously upped her fitness regime when COVID-19 hit. The first day she arrived back on campus, a male colleague she'd not seen for a year or so crossed the street and remarked, "Wow, you look great! You've de-aged—you want to be careful they don't demote you as well!" "Professors can't look like young women?" Simone enquired. "They don't often look like women!" said her interlocutor. "Good on you for expanding the category," he added nervously as he bade her a hasty "good morning." Both Alison and Simone have been baffled and thrown by remarks like these that, when parsed in a certain way, contain the seeds of a knowledge that something is wrong: women shouldn't be hired on the basis of how they look; we should not assume that we need to add "woman" as a qualifier to "professor." They also contain the weaponry to diminish and attack women: young attractive women don't fit the categories they occupy; pretty women can never be taken seriously.

Parinaz's photograph does not represent as a single, outrageous case. A recent article published in the *Journal of Vascular Surgery* entitled "Prevalence of Unprofessional Social Media Content among Young Vascular Surgeons" was authored by a nearly all-male research team. It sought to classify the behaviour of vascular surgery students on social media as either professional or unprofessional with one criterion: "provocative attire" as worn by women doctors. The only female member of the team justified this, remarking, "People get judged every day by what is available on social media in all forms. It is the reality of today's world in medicine or any other profession, like it or not." The article has since been retracted.

While a range of responses was offered up to Parinaz's allegedly pro-vocative photograph, there is singular exclusivity here, too, in the sense that such a situation was highly unlikely to happen to men. Indeed, our female interlocutors often took the view that their bodies registered the effects of the patriarchy in ways that male bodies did not.

The mentoring advice dispensed to Annabel in the women-only promotion sessions alerted us as to how gains might be made for women by, effectively, replicating the habits, accoutrements, and *techniques du corps* of men; in this way, being read as a woman, as Annabel might be, or as Parinaz was, could be avoided; instead, they could place themselves on the same playing field as men. The leader of the women-only promotion sessions began with this very notion, saying how sick and tired she was of seeing women turning up to interviews and speaking about their roles in "passive" ways. She wondered aloud if women knew just how common it was for them to appear with slouched shoulders and bowed heads, or with low voices or voices pitched too loud and delivering words too fast. She also wondered if the assembled attendees knew how common it was for women to distribute credit for work among others, and to background their work with passive expressions. "I want to hear active verbs!" she implored. "Men have no trouble doing this! Claim what it is that you do."

The session leader certainly had a point; we know only too well from femi-nist writing that responsibility for action can be rendered invisible when an actor goes unnamed. As Jackson Katz notes,

> We speak about how many women were raped in the last year, almost never of how many men were convicted of rape offences; we speak of how many teen-aged girls got pregnant, almost never of how many boys impregnated teenaged girls (2017:np).

While we are not at all enamoured with Katz's expression, that (ironically) indicates the activity of pregnancy is made by males in the act of "impregnat-ing," we want to underscore his point: that the passive voice has a political effect. The online resource *Language: A Feminist Guide* called on the media at large in 2014 to abandon the passive in favour of active-voice headlines that properly ascribed activity for which actants could be held responsible, such as "Man rapes woman dog-walker," instead of "Woman raped while walking dog." The resource notes that the politics of passivity were made plain by George Orwell in his 1946 essay "Politics and the English Language," which advised "never use the passive where you can use the active" (Orwell, 1946: 139). Instead of making this advisement on the basis that it was poor style,

Orwell included it on a list of rules for combatting the politically motivated abuse of language, naming it as a tool wielded by the powerful to conceal inconvenient or unpalatable truths and for the manipulation of public opinion. Agentless passives are also common in legal proceedings, and in that context the feminist argument has some force. Ehrlich (2001) notes that "the grammar of non-agency" is politically leveraged in legal contexts. Citing cases in which men who have been accused of sexual violence, Ehrlich notes that the lawyers who represent those men very often make strategic use of agentless passives. In her book *Representing Rape*, Ehrlich analyses a sexual assault trial in which the defense lawyer asks his client questions like, "I take it the sweater was removed?" It's not hard to see what the lawyer hopes to achieve by choosing an agentless construction that refuses to specify who removed the sweater. If the court is of the view that the complainant took off her own clothes, that will support—or at least, not contradict—the defense's argument that she consented to sex. As Ehrlich says, it is only to be expected that defendants and their lawyers will use this strategy. It is more surprising, and more worrying, that the same tendency to downplay men's agency has been observed in the language used by judges. When Coates and Wade (2014) analysed the language used in judgments on sexual assault cases in Western Canada, they found many examples of judges using agentless passives like this:

> "There was advantage taken of a situation that presented itself." This statement was made in the judgment on a case where a ten year-old girl had been sexually assaulted by a stranger in her home. The "situation," in other words, was the presence of a child in her own bedroom, and it did not magically "present itself," it was engineered by the defendant. A jury had found the defendant guilty, but the judge chose to minimize the seriousness of his offence by describing it in a way that implied he had no agency at all—as if he merely reacted, as anyone might, to the circumstances in which he (inexplicably) found himself. The judge's statement is an egregious example of "the grammar of non-agency" (2014: 12).

On this basis that the women-only promotion sessions implore women to reclaim what is lost in and through their own agent deletion; that their bodies and activity might disappear, be erased by the overriding presence of male dominance. This erasure is a wholesale one, made by patriarchal means according to the session leader, who remarked "the university is serious about turning the patriarchy on its head—we want you to succeed, and you have to know what you're up against and how to combat it." The changes ushered in require individuals to shine, to create records of their own that result in measurable success. In team situations, as Blackmore (2015) notes, this is difficult, because accrued points for research outputs must be divided in the accounting systems ushered in via the Dawkins reforms. Thus, team research that best meets endorsed research goals must be balanced against the need to accrue the evidence of individual successes. This tension is writ large in promotion contexts where the individual must accrue as much evidence as possible to furnish their own case for performance success demonstrated against such measures. The disappearance of women in collectivity in the everyday use of "*we*" required correction; and that required mimicking male strategies for the reassertion of the "*I.*" Neoliberal economic rationality privileges autonomy and competition that individualises responsibility for success or failure (Blackmore, 2014; Ahmed, 2012; Davies & Bansel, 2010); self-promotion and self-surveillance are absolutely required in this paradigm (Hey & Bradford, 2004). As Acker (1990) and Bailyn (2003) each observe, such concepts and practices are not gender neutral, but are firmly tied to white heteronormative mythologies and practices of institutional work. As Bailyn notes:

> the academy is anchored in assumptions about competence and success that have led to practices and norms constructed around the life experiences of men, and around a vision of masculinity as the normal, universal requirement of university life (2003: 143).

Feminist critics of mentoring programs that advise women to adopt the strategies of male dominance (e.g., Devos, 2008; Colley, 2003; Ely & Meyerson, 2000) have recognised how such strategies make women responsible for their own inclusion in systems that discriminate against them and leave the game and its rules wholly intact.

It would be folly, however, to see the recommended use of mimicry of men, as was advised in the women-only mentoring session, as a strategic means of achieving gender equity as straightforwardly self-defeating. As Bhabha (1994) notes, mimicry is a kind of double vision. Mimicry depends on the presence of (here) he who is mimicked, but equally disrupts its authority; the mimicry is never quite the same. In its slight deviations lie possibilities for reworking that which is mimicked. Such reworkings might be achieved in and through incrementally "turning the patriarchy on its head," as the leader of the women-only promotion session leader desired for her assembled female audience. In such a circumstance, the mimicry of women would have trumped the original, male performance: women could use male strategies to beat men at their own game. We will return to this potentiality of mimicry momentarily, suggesting that even though it is replete with potential, there is not much that can be done to realise it, within the confines of neoliberal participation.

CORPOREAL ACCOUNTING

Alternative models of mentoring seek to divorce such dominating institutional interests from the substantive matter of elevating women in the institution by calling for a recognition and valuing of gendered differences. One such revaluation of the feminine that emphasizes female difference involves a concessionary form of corporeal accounting. This is also something we found operational in our own institution—and we privilege Alison's own experience in what follows to draw it out.

Corporeal accounting appeared in ethnographic enquiry as the only available strategy for dealing with the impact of caring responsibilities, still borne principally by women. Facility is provided in competitive grants applications to detail one's "Research Opportunity and Performance Evidence" (ROPE). In the ROPE section of an Australian Research Council application, aspirants detail any extenuating circumstances that have presented disruption, interruption, or delay (see Klocker & Drozdzewski, 2012). The section is designed to make plain the differential access that applicants have to opportunity— whether by reason of illness, caring responsibilities, misadventure, childbirth and childcare, and so on. As Dalton (2011) notes, while opportunity to document interruptions and delays permits the recognition that women are disproportionately impacted by career disruptions (like childbirth, caring for others, domestic violence) there is no point at which a challenge to the implied singular norm from which deviation is made (Dalton, 2011: 5). Rafferty (2010) and Klocker and Drozdzewski (2012) point out that while visibility of women's circumstances might be achieved, no changes to expected standards of performance are in the offing. The best that can be hoped for is that something less than the expected standard will be excused. Yet, numbers of publications and funding dollars excused still stand on one's record as unachieved. Fewer publications often mean less opportunity for promotion, less capacity to appear competitive in the grants arena.

The imbalance in research output that often results might influence promotion, and not always in entirely expected ways. Therese, an Australian social scientist, was hoping to achieve the rank of associate professor in a scheduled promotion round at her institution. She was worried, though, because she had been "on an 80 percent research arrangement" as a result of the grants she held; this had exempted her from all but the lightest of teaching and service duties. She told Simone that she might be "a little stressed" about demonstrating in her application that she had produced a higher number of quality research outputs, housed in the right scholarly outlets, than those on standard research and teaching contracts. On balance, and on the advice of others to whom she had sent her application, Therese felt "pretty confident." What she was really worried about was that she did not have any career disruptions to speak of; especially pertinent was that she did not have a child. "Fuck. I can't fall back on family," she lamented to Simone.

> That's the one thing I could really use. I'm single, I've got no babies. By choice. I worry that I'll be read as someone who should be using all my time to do research. I basically did [do that], but it would be excellent to have a buffer.

Therese's is not, perhaps, a common reason for delaying or avoiding applying for promotion; hers is an interesting counter case that demonstrates just how engrained is the idea of a male standard, from which females are generally considered to deviate.

New regimes of research production have presumed a male standard academic figure; care represents a deviation from it. This deviation must be explained in order to excuse or account for a failure to achieve a timely ascendency up the ranks (see Pillay, Kluvers, Abhayawansa & Vedran, 2013). The impact of caring, too, on the travel that might be necessitated by research projects involving field or archival research has been explored; women lose out here, being more bound to place as a result of caring responsibilities (see Menzies & Newson, 2008).

Alison is particularly well acquainted with this problem, having been confined to the time and space coordinates determined by the needs of her baby son and young daughters. Mobility, she found, was necessary in acquiring capital in the global knowledge economy—to attend conferences, to develop research collaborations, to develop the skills, expertise and attributes that indicate international standing, all of which are required to gain promotion to the professoriate (see for example Boden & Epstein, 2006). Alison found herself having to forego such opportunities because she could not (and did not want to) relinquish her responsibilities to her young family. The acquisition of international standing could be problematic, too, for academics who did not have the financial capacity to attend conferences unless they had secured supporting funds. Especially if one did not yet have a suitably impressive track record as a junior academic, such funds might be hard to get, and one's own discretionary research funds might not be sufficient—or even existent—to support such crucial activity.

As Bell and Bentley note,

> the increased scope, scale and depth of what constitutes research leadership means track record "relative to opportunity" that recognises women's broken career trajectories is often ignored in committees where sustained track record dominates. Having children is not the norm. Yet: life choices (to delay entering the academy, to undertake periods of part-time or casual work, to commence

a career as a research assistant, to have children, to care for aging parents) do not alter one's capacity to produce high quality research outcomes, nor indeed to produce "breakthrough research," but they may impact on the quantum of research productivity, the strength of research networks and mentors, professional mobility and therefore profile (2005: 1).

The difference of women's bodies is here writ large, and problematic. Alison is particularly vexed by the biological presumptions that underpin gendered bodies, noting that ideas about women's social and emotional vulnerabilities are based in faulty understandings of the differences between female and male biologies. She notes in particular here that the idea that men are universally stronger and more resilient to harm than are females has been disproven in studies of core skeletal makeup that show men and women have the same quality of bone and rate of degradation as we age (Tommasini, Nasser & Jepsen, 2007). This makes women no more vulnerable than men in absolute physical terms—and, by extension, social terms.

Despite Alison's strenuous and outraged objections, there exists a male standard of academic performance that has been critically engaged in the form of offering concessions to women when, for reasons of their femininity, they depart from expectations based on the male standard. An example emerged when we spoke with Mariana, an Australian anthropologist in her late forties. "Ohhhh, it's a roller coaster ride," said Mariana of being an academic. She elaborated,

> I dread that awful, awful feeling of being behind—which I almost always am, just because I tell myself that lie, that I work best under pressure and instead of catching up on the work stuff for the whole weekend I might spend a day in the garden or loafing in front of the telly with a wine. Then the pressure is on. I don't think I'm lazy. I'm not. But I do resent that whole thing of living to work instead of working to live, but what we do isn't nine to five, ever. If you add a service role or two to that and some PhD students, and you teach and research, well, there isn't any chance you get weekends and evenings off, is there? Oh, and kids on top of that—and a partner—whoever he is. I barely see him. And all of that makes me feel really low. But then I get these incredible highs, such as when I'm chasing down an idea and solving a tricky problem in a paper. And when I'm at a conference and giving a paper that is well received and that I'm proud of, or when after months of work you score that big grant money. They're better than any recreational drug, hands down. Am I worse off than a bloke here? she continued. Oh fuck, yeah. I had the babies, I took the mat leave, I had the career interruptions. It feels like you have to apologise for this weakness and see if they will forgive you for it. I actually had someone ask me when I went for an RA position—I mean granted, it was over two decades ago—if I planned to have children during the research period because the CIs didn't want to have to replace the person they chose. How are you supposed to respond to that—do you

say, "sorry I have a body that can get knocked up, I'll try ever so hard to control it for you," or do you tell them you'll be the one to chose when and if you reproduce and it won't have anything to do with their schedule, or do you ask them if they know how children are made and point out that men also become parents? Or that pregnancy is not an illness and you could probably work even if you were having a child? I actually wound up telling them that I had gone through very skilled transgender surgery and I was thrilled they thought I looked so much like a woman. I didn't get that gig, unsurprisingly!

A particular mathematics of biosocial labour was available to Mariana when she totted up the hours, days, weeks, months or years of "interruption" that exempted her from the standard assessment of output and activity that would otherwise be expected of her. Concessionary approaches reveal just how entailed what "standard" is; pregnancy, for instance, is a deviation from standard, not itself standard.

Alison and Simone have each produced mathematical explanations to justify their own departures from male standards. For one submission of an Australian Research Council grant, Simone received reassurance of the robustness of her academic record from a senior woman mentor whom she had asked to look over her application prior to submission. However, she was advised to nevertheless include her parental care duties because "you'll be judged against men who didn't have to do that; you want to be sure the assessors read your application knowing you've been held up. There could have been another couple of papers if you hadn't been otherwise occupied." Alison was similarly advised, with even more pointed counsel. Her mentor cautioned her *not* to say on her promotion application, "I had a baby, but I still did X, Y and Z." She was advised instead to say, "I did X, Y and Z and also had a baby." The latter was advised so that attention was not drawn to the fact that Alison had taken time off to raise babies; the idea was to point out that she had managed to meet the male standard and also have a baby, thus *exceeding* expectations. Simone totted up exactly how much time she had spent attending to the needs of her child to quantify her deviation from the male standard of performance expectations. Alison worked on the word order of her promotion interview. While each of their advisors had offered them ways to level the playing field, the advice itself served to reinforce the fact that maternity constituted a deviation from the male norm.

Processes of corporeal accounting could sometimes be called out as unfair accounting for advantage. One of our interviewees, Bella, a humanities lecturer in Australia, disclosed how she had been discussing inequality in a staff meeting and was asked by a senior male academic to "stop playing the baby card." Bella was "shocked" and said she felt,

Quite hurt. This was someone with kids. But he was very clearly not on my side. He had a different experience of childrearing, which is fine, but do not discount my experience because it is more involved than yours, by which I mean I have children actually feeding from my body making it a lot harder to go to conferences or on fieldwork and I should have a right to try to fix that.

"Fixing it" meant going through calculative processes of exemption that put women like Bella in situations where they could stand accused of rorting the system and diddling the numbers. Women had to be careful to reflect their deviations from male standards and be mindful of the impacts of doing so. Alison, for example, was cautioned not to include information in a grant application regarding her experiences of miscarriage or IVF because, in the words of one of her own mentors, it would be viewed as a "sob story" and a ploy for attention that would see her caught out diddling the numbers.

The need to produce careful corporeally based numbers of exemption also impacted women who did not have, and did not want, children. Ingrid, a young female academic at an Australian Institution disclosed to Alison,

I feel like I need to regularly overproduce and do amazing things to almost apologise for the fact I do not have any bouts of maternity leave to account for why I haven't done more than men at my same level.

There are clearly significant pressures bearing down on women to make themselves as close to the male standard as possible. The consequences of not doing so might be high: failure to secure a grant or a promotion may ensue for a woman if she does not detail the circumstances of her deviation and properly account for it.

As the examples of maternity we have reviewed here demonstrate—including cases of women electing not to have children—women's difference is never fully convertible to the male standard. Simone's mentor clearly suggested this when she advised Simone to "play the parental card," even though Simone did not need to—so that her publications accomplishments would look even better on a grant application. The terms of the game could be pressed for advantage so that the capital of greatest worth could be accrued to Simone's best advantage. This mentoring advisement was underscored by the idea that in their very failure to fully conform to the standard, women's bodies present a significant challenge to the patriarchal organisation of the institution. Their difference means they could never be fully brought under the control of patriarchal institutions, and they could use their difference to gain advantage. Sometimes they might be able to surpass it by saying, as Alison was advised to say, "I achieved the standard and I had a baby."

But, in situations where power is generated "in and through the reproduction of structures of domination" (Giddens, 1981: 4) women could do little but involve and entail themselves in existing patriarchal structures, by way of imitation. Even though corporeal accounting methods might be utilised to show that women could beat men at their own game, the accounting could not be emancipatory because the game had not changed. Rachel, a Canadian geoscience assistant professor in her early thirties knew the conditions of the game were against her. Rachel described to Simone the advice she had been given by her mentor, to imitate male style in her work attire, lest the principal way in which she was perceived was "as a woman." Her mentor had intended to provide guidance that reduced the possibility that Rachel's work could take a back seat to her gender—her work should be why Rachel was noticed. Advised by her mentor to "dress androgynously," Rachel remarked that, even though she had followed the advice of her mentor, the guidance had produced the effect of "Imposter syndrome. It gives me headaches and sometimes I feel nauseous about work." She commented that, in an office space

> fairly heaving with penises it is hard to miss I'm the odd man out—and I mean "odd man" because I kind of have to act like a man of sorts to fit in. No makeup and dresses for me here. They might think I'll cry or don't want to get my hands dirty—or worse, they'll think I'm the secretary. I wear pants and I exude a confident, capable vibe that I wear like clothes. That all comes off when I get home. And sometimes, yes, I do cry there.

All too familiar with the conditions under which crying could occur, and the ways in which tears could constitute a serious departure from a standard "work demeanour," Alison immediately related to Rachel's situation. Alison intuitively knew that crying was tied to femininity, and she knew it in two ways. As a biological anthropologist and as a mother with a young baby, Alison knew that crying was a biological reflex that women are more prone to exhibit during increased prolactin production. She also knew that crying at work could have ramifications. On bereavement leave, Alison was unexpectedly called into the office for an urgent meeting. She attended, but, overwhelmed, she couldn't hold back her tears and cried during the meeting. Doing so brought Alison no relief as she worried, for weeks, about how her tears would impact how she was understood at work: she feared it was as a weak leader, deviant from the expected standard. It did not occur to her until much later that the male colleague who had summonsed her for the meeting would likely have no such concerns about his own performance: *she* was the one who had cried and departed from the expected emotional demeanour.[5]

It is interesting that both Alison and Rachel referenced the very old patriarchal ideology of separate male and female spheres; an idea traceable to the Aristotelian distinguishment between the (male) sphere of *polis* and the (female) sphere of *oikos*. Formalised in the Industrial Revolution, male and female participation in public and private spheres respectively is based in biologically determined gender roles that restrict women from full participation in the domains of politics, industry, commerce and law. It struck Simone that advisements given to both women with respect to dress, emotional demeanour and maternity, and the horror both felt about the prospect of crying at work referenced these spheres and required the transmogrification of female bearing into male on entry to the public sphere. When the magical transformation brought about by donning male accoutrement, speech and bearing failed to sustain itself, female bodies revealed themselves to be imposters. Imitation slipped; females were exposed beneath the outfits that were only costumes. Moments of affective transgression, like crying, and female responses to them reveal the deeply gendered institutional norms of demeanour and the ways in which they have been internalised, as "weak," or inappropriate. They also reveal the limits of imitation for bringing about gender equity goals, even when women beat men at their own game. The old Aristotelian divisions remain firmly cleaved, if deviations—like crying—are still perceived precisely as such.[6] That is, slippages must be mastered, rather than critically questioned. Mentor advisements on what to wear, how to walk, how to talk require mastery, skilled imitation, of the ideal form.

Hacker (2018) notes that the ideal form is that one ought not to cry: there is "little room for crying" in universities; it only reinforces patriarchal perceptions of hierarchical essentialist differences between the sexes (Hacker, 2018: 282). But such remarks fail to appreciate the perniciousness of neoliberal institutional arenas in which, for example, as Newman (2013) argues, "emotional intelligence," "empathy" and "humanisation" are all valuable assets attached umbilically to women, who "soften" institutional relations and structures (2013: 207). Crying may not straightforwardly indicate a falling out of the taken-for-granted incorporation of the patriarchal institutional landscape, as sociologist Jack Katz might suggest (see 1999: 332); neoliberalist structures are too expansive for a fall entirely "out" of them to be accomplished. The significance of one's situated conduct, which Katz argues comes home to people when they "fall out" of context might be initially misrecognised as "women's weakness," compared with men's emotional toughness. But neoliberal operations assign value to these apparent weaknesses and leverage them for gain. There is certainly no shortage of literature detailing the value of the "humanising," "empathetic," or "understanding" touch of a woman; the funeral industry has long known how to leverage such qualities to create and dominate a gap in the male-dominated industry, in which strength, resilience and bearing up have been the emotional mainstays (see for example

Donley & Baird, 2017). Now, human resource gurus fully conversant in the language of "emotional intelligence" and its value to new managerialism provide foundational gendered rationalisation for female participation in the institution. Harding, Ford and Fotaki (2013), for example, describe how differences between men and women are made to appear "natural," and therefore unassailable. These differences manifest as structural norms and emerge as key organisational features. Included here are ideas about the greater female capacity for nurturance and care, as befits the best teachers, and the idea that women are good at resolving conflicts—making them exceptionally effective middle managers and advisors to executive level (male) leaders. Crying is no failed mimicry; it's an exploitable opportunity in neoliberalist context.

NOTES

1. There are limited opportunities to grow exponentially in its location in Australia's compact capital city that, while lovely if you enjoy the aesthetic of socialism done stylishly right—is hardly a drawcard for young undergraduates. There used to be a running joke at the ANU; insiders liked to call it the ALU instead: Australia's *Local* University. That held for undergraduates, who were typically the children of the three main employers in town: the public service (and other service folk, including diplomats), armed forces and university staff. Postgraduate and doctoral students, however, know the university's reputation: it is the best in Australia and consistently in the top twenty-five universities in the world. Our own discipline of Anthropology was, at time of writing, ranked fourth in the world.

2. Somewhat curiously, the CSIRO still exists, even though its role could easily be understood as replicating what universities do. Indeed, it has been something of a go-to for university staff members like Simone, who are interested in the tools CSIRO uses to justify activity on public funds.

3. This exposure is now a dire imperilment referred to as an "overexposure" for many universities since the rise of COVID-19, which will indubitably see some universities—or parts of them—cease to exist.

4. The methods governments used to pursue their objectives changed in the 1970s in an attendance to more accountable management. As Marginson and Considine (2000) note, this was not immediately successful. The Keynesian model of the postwar period had presumed that governments could bring about changes in the behaviours of organisations by manipulating demand and supply. But if organisations did not respond to those levers, or if they did not achieve the intended objectives, not much could be done. But a new model of public management emerged: the interested reader may consult Marginson and Considine (2000: 40).

5. American journalist and author Anne Kreamer, who specializes in business, work/life balance, culture, and women's issues and writes about them in her numerous books and in the *Harvard Business Review,* made a study of crying at work in 2011. In a study of US workplaces, Kreamer found that 41 percent of women have

cried at work compared to just 9 percent of men. She found that when men cried at work, they felt better, but women felt worse, usually as a result of worrying over the impacts of having done so, as Alison had. Kreamer ties such experiences directly to the operations of patriarchal structures, noting that worrying about crying was caused by underlying imposter syndrome.

6. Both Gunn (2010) and Campbell (1998) contend that masculine speech is the cultural standard. It's what we value and respect. The low pitch and assertive demeanour that characterize the adult male voice signify reason, control and authority, suitable for the public domain. Women's voices are higher pitched, like those of immature boys, and their characteristic speech patterns have a distinctive cadence that exhibits a wider range of emotional expression. In Western cultures, contends Gunn, this is bad because it comes across as uncontrolled. We associate uncontrolled speech (what Gunn calls "the cry, the grunt, the scream, and the yawp") with bodily functions and sexuality—things that happen in the private, domestic spheres (both coded as feminine). Men are expected to repress passionate, emotional speech, Gunn explains, precisely because it threatens norms of masculine control and order.

Chapter 3

Interlude: A Short Note about Secret Transparencies

In the previous chapter, we unmasked the kinds of secrets the neoliberal university keeps—secrets that are hidden away behind activities that ostensibly bolster and support women. We argued that activities like running women-only mentoring sessions that teach women to walk and talk like men really only reinforce a male standard; they make women engage in a game of imitation that they cannot win, even when they best gold-standard male performances. They cannot win because the foundational rational actor in neoliberal operations is invariably imagined to be male. We demonstrated that females—by virtue of their biology and the sociocultural circumstances of their gendered being—must account for valid deviations from this foundational man in order to be excused, but not exempted, from institutional and other expectations. As Blackmore (2014), Ahmed (2012), and Davies and Bansel (2010) point out, the autonomy, competition and entrepreneurialism required in neoliberal economic practice is easier to produce for some bodies than it is for others (see for example David, 2014; Ahmed, 2012; Slaughter & Leslie, 1997). They are especially difficult to produce for bodies that must stay in a tight orbit around children and others requiring care, for pregnant bodies, and bodies subject to all manner of violences.

As Clare Birchall (2011) has observed, looking for institutional secrets is a conventional analysis to make of the neoliberal entity. She notes that analysts tend to favour secrets—that is, they set aside all of the really obvious and evident things that, in our case, the university might say about gender equity in favour of an exploration of what the university might be secreting away behind that claim.

This tendency to look behind what is declared is writ large in the case of universities and gender equity because, when compared to the evident sexism of the bad old days, the present situation seems a radical improvement, and the subtler—but no less grievous—forms of institutional sexism can go unnoticed. Analysis of gender equity is thus in the business of peeling back institutional obfuscation to get to the rotten secrets that dwell beneath glossy veneers (see for example Black & Garvis, 2018; Gannon et al., 2015; Bagihole & White, 2013; Petersen, 2009; Blackmore & Sachs, 2007).

Rotten secrets include, as Harding, Ford and Fotaki (2013) note, the way in which differences between men and women are made to appear "natural" in the neoliberal institution, and so their effects—including the use of women to "humanise" and "soften" the institution—go unnoticed. They include, too, as Bailyn (2003) notes, how claims of gender, ethnic and sexual neutrality are actually heavily male biased—as the material in our last chapter shows. These analysts set aside what institutions say in favour of ferreting out the secrets that sit behind their statements. Typically, these analysts do exactly as we did in our last chapter: they push behind what look like supportive ideas and practices and show just how biased they might actually be against female success.

But, as Birchall says, there is great benefit in exploring, rather than tossing aside, the screens behind which secrets are presumed to lurk. This is especially true when universities say things about their practice that are not all that flattering. Here, perhaps most interesting about what universities have to say about gender equity is the *transparency* of the remarks. Our own institution, for example, does not mince words at all when it comes to declaring just how far behind the institution is when it comes to gender equity. Indeed, ANU has been extremely forthright in declaring the lamentable situation of female oppression. It openly admits its gender equity failings in public remarks like these:

> Over recent years the University has made some progress on gender equity, however we recognise that there is more to be done. [At the ANU] there is still a high gender imbalance amongst academic staff, with around twice as many men as women. About half of the University's PhD graduates are women, but just one quarter of senior academics at ANU are women. The loss of so many women from the career pipeline is a waste of talent, and negatively impacts our capacity for world-class research and innovation (Australian National University, 2019b).

Remarks such as these exemplify transparency; that tendency towards disclosure, that indication of honesty and of having nothing to hide. Tobacco companies have fully embraced transparency, too, frankly declaring that combustible tobacco will harm and even kill humans. As they (and Simone) certainly know, transparency can have the same effects as secrecy: secrecy can flourish beautifully in "transparent" realms.[1] As they also know, there is a great deal of capital to be extracted from being transparent (see Dennis, 2016). Noting that "transparency is a virtue," Birchall (2011: 8) argues that transparency is a key sign of cultural and moral authority. By operating it, especially in the form of full disclosure about things like gender disparities, institutions can claim "transparency capital." She observes that,

> particularly when it comes to government actions and accounts, the moral discourse that condemns secrecy and rewards transparency may cause us to overlook the integral, perhaps constitutive, role secrecy (in different guises) might play (2011: 13).

With clear reference to Derrida (2001), Birchall goes on to remark that getting transparency right is difficult:

> A regime that embraces transparency will only ever be able to go so far before it tips over into totalitarianism because of its parallels with surveillance, particularly when extended to citizens. Resisting the call to be transparent to the state is, then, automatically registered as a sign of guilt. But if the regime doesn't go far enough, if it shrinks back from applying transparency to its own actions, the regime meets the charge of totalitarianism coming the other way (for acting covertly, autonomously and without an explicit mandate). Hence an infinite hesitation, a radical undecidability, within any democracy that counts transparency among its operating principles. Hence too the prospect of a debate between transparency and secrecy that will never be concluded, because far from being inimical to each other, they are symbiotic. This is why the stakes of that debate are so routinely misunderstood. It's not a question of reframing the supposed opposition between transparency and secrecy in ever wider perspectives, because such reframing assumes that the terms can be made to yield to interpretive mastery (2011: 12).

In terms of organizational strategy, all levels of institutional practice tend toward transparency—pay scales, promotions criteria, and essay marking matrices are all published. Processes, procedures, policies, governance structures, financial data are all shared with institutional members, thus satisfying calls for organisational accountability. However, none of that presentation of institutional practice is (a) necessarily devoid of secrecy, and (b) none of it is necessarily neutral.

Of neutrality, we suggest, as Richards (1993) does of colonialist practice, that one at least partially controls geographic territory by engaging in the political act of "producing, distributing, and consuming information about it" (Richards, 1993: 17).[2] In our next chapter, we suggest something similar when we explore how the institution produces information about gender disparity. As part of its production, the institution of the Australian National University suggests that the university campus bears the historical legacy of male dominance in its named buildings. It suggests that by naming more buildings after prominent and accomplished university women, that patriarchal architectural legacy can be consigned to the past: the signal can be sent that the built campus represents the importance of women.

The institution isn't trying to hide anything here; it recognises the problem, proposes a solution and sets about rectifying a pressing and consequential barrier to female institutional participation. What is hidden in the very declaration of problem and solution, however, are the terms of the naming—as we show in the following chapter. We argue therein that something important is made opaque in the very transparency with which gender inequity is described and addressed.

In the context of a university (or a government) there are countless ways to make the appearance of transparency without ever actually shifting away from opacity, without ever having to give away secrets. The provision of incomprehensible data comes instantly to mind; something about which academics complain ceaselessly at our own institution. The information is there, and it is usually presented in just the ways we might expect. But it might leave certain calculations out of the final figures. The figures might not be explicated, so we can't really know exactly what they indicate. Or, they might depend entirely for their context on other numbers that do not exist in the same area—and a person might have to have some nous, some background knowledge, or even some especial clearance level to be able to access where to look for them. In the case of the buildings and the participation in gender equity programs we discuss in our next chapter, the institutionally provided information is certainly not incomprehensible. It is, however, darkly opaque, effectively shrouding deeply gendered histories, politics and labour imbalances.

With these ideas in mind we stay with institutional narratives in the next chapter, looking at the ways in which their very *dis*closures contain within them the *en*closure of women to patriarchal histories and politics.

NOTES

1. As Birchall (2011) notes, the so-called knowledge economy, not least because of the way in which it puts a premium on being "in the know" or possessing the secret, is another domain characterized by a tension between transparency and secrecy.

2. This is as true for imperialists as it is for contemporary Western governments, where secrecy means impropriety and transparency means the end of the controlling monopoly, the end of corruption, freedom of information, accountability, and the idea that the government and its business belong to, and are essentially of, the people (see for example Schmitt, 2010).

Chapter 4

Haunted by the Undead Patriarchy

New Buildings, SWAN Songs, and Secrets

ATHENA'S ORIENTATION

Just as Athena once appeared to the young Telemachus as a beautiful, statuesque and accomplished woman, in this chapter she appears to the Australian National University's women as a tall, beautiful building. In this guise she offers insight into the state of the university in respect to gender relations, for she arrives at a point of time when the tall and beautiful building is to be given a woman's name. The goddess also makes a special appearance as herself—in the form of Athena SWAN.

In this chapter, we examine institutional stories that are told about the patriarchy. We look at their transparent claims, teasing out how they contain within them the "secrets" of female oppression, even though institutional remarks deride it and seek to demonstrate, always, its ever-diminishing presence. We trace, too, the declared imminence of death of the patriarchy. The patriarchy is not dead, but it was, according to our participants, not robustly alive, either. It is strong, still, but it isn't like it used to be; women might not have pay parity and might have to treat pregnancy as a career setback, but they could not be excluded from supervising a student on the basis of their gender, as Marie Reay, a former ANU employee with a new building named after her, had once been. The patriarchy was someplace in between dead and alive. It lingers on, still making its effects keenly felt, but it could not be said to be as vigorous as it once was. We trace that betwixtness of male institutional dominance in this chapter, arguing that its lingering continuance between force to be reckoned with and consignment to the past gives rise to a very productive space, one in which named mentoring programs thrive. In the context of rising female institutional participation, women can feel victorious; much has been won. But there is yet a good deal yet to accomplish, as the fullness of gender equity cannot yet be said to have come to pass. These betwixt conditions are fertile for establishing the validity of mentoring, and for setting its equity agendas. We argue in this chapter that in the liminal zone where nothing and no one clearly reigns supreme, structured mentoring practices tend to take on the very patriarchal forms of governance over women that they abhor.

PATRIARCHAL STORIES

Patriarchy is a complex, complicated term deployed in multiple ways. Our analysis of key institutional stories reveals that a new period of gender equity is not nearly as well established and operational as institutional stories claim. Neither is "the patriarchy" firmly entrenched—even though its consequential effects are still keenly, practically felt. Rather, a liminal period in which neither is paradigmatically established is in play. We cite here a looming danger besetting a key desire of mentoring programs: to establish a new order of gender equity. In the long, drawn-out period in which the patriarchy lingers on and on—not dead, and not fully alive—mentoring practice can take on, mimetically replicate, its structures. We point to the ways in which its own hierarchical structuring may re-present, rather than simply copying, existing patriarchal relations. In our investigation of how understandings of patriarchy are disseminated, taken up, rejected and reworked, we take the view that Hannah Arendt did when she suggested that the "political" is best understood as a power relation between private and public realms, and that storytelling is a vital bridge between these realms—a site where individualized passions and shared perspectives are contested and interwoven (see Arendt, 1998). This insight provided the impetus for Jackson's 2002 work *The Politics of Storytelling.* Therein, Jackson explores and expands these Arentian notions through a cross-cultural analysis of storytelling that includes Kuranko stories from Sierra Leone, Aboriginal stories of the stolen generation, stories recounted before the South African Truth and Reconciliation Commission, and stories of refugees, renegades, and war veterans. The common theme arising from them is violence, within which especial attention is given to the volatile conditions under which stories are (and are not) told. In Jackson's take on things, the narrative reworkings of "reality" enable people to symbolically alter subject-object relations. This permits variously located tellers, re-tellers and audiences, intended and unintended, of stories to restore existential viability to the intersubjective fields of self and other, self and state, self and situation. We follow Jackson in this line of thinking, but abandon the notion that narrative remains a whole and choate force in the processes he describes in favour of an infiltration of experience that means feelingful experience orders and rearranges story as much as, if not more compellingly than, narrative and counter narrative. We focus instead on how the institution declares, matter of factly, how dire things are for gender equity. That is, we focus on a particular kind of story: the story of transparency.

What is in these apparently transparent declarations? In their very transparency lie the secrets of female institutional disadvantage. In this chapter, for instance, we show how the declaration that a new campus building will be named after a remarkable woman, to help correct male institutional representation, is in fact a deeply patriarchal act. There is no need to set aside transparent institutional statements, for they are very telling. As we indicated in the short interlude preceding this chapter, the trend, especially in respect to feminist scholarship, has been to dismiss what the institution says as a coverup, set those statements aside, and then hunt for the secret they obscure. This is not to suggest that there are not secrets (like naturalising women's institutional contributions on the basis of their presumed biological and emotional capacities or proposing gender neutrality in processes that are in fact tilted against female success). It is instead to suggest that secrets are often entailed in transparency, rather than concealed entirely behind them.

STORIES OF SPACE MEN

The first kind of story we want to tell is, perhaps unusually, spatial. During our fieldwork, a new precinct called Kambri[1]—one of five new hubs—was (very rapidly) constructed and opened at the ANU campus. The new precinct is part of the largest development since the ANU's inception and is part of a strategic commitment to create an unrivalled campus environment, as described under its new Campus Master Plan. In his 2019 State of the University (Chancellor's Speech) the ANU's then Chancellor, Gareth Evans, described how the Plan would focus on:

> concentrating new development around five clearly defined hubs (of which Kambri will be just one), creating distinctive new gateways to the university (fousing particularly on University Avenue), bringing greater harmony and elegance to our future architecture, transforming the circulation system by pushing out cars to the perimeter and giving primacy in the centre to pedestrians and bikes, and making far more than we ever have before of ANU's greatest physical asset, our fabulous natural bush setting (Evans, 2019).

The need to create an unrivalled campus environment arose because of ANU's aforementioned overall plan, to become "the Oxbridge of the South," as the vice chancellor quipped in a 2020 piece in *The Australian* newspaper. Of course, things were moving ahead with much greater spirit and rapidity before COVID-19, devastating bushfires and freak hailstorms all arrived in the summer of 2019/2020 to reorient everyone to the devastating financial and infrastructural legacies of convergent crises. In common with other university campuses across Australia, buildings works have ceased as universities limit expenditures.

The plan, which, depending on the university's recovery, is to be made manifest over the next twenty years, will indubitably transform the campus space. But Chancellor Evans also recognised something else in his remarks: the lurking propensity of matters spatial to violence. While at the time of his speech Evans could not have had any inkling of the physical violence that was about to be unleashed *on* the university campus in the form of hail and fire, he did know at the time of some other violences that had arisen as a result *of* the particular campus space. Evans (2019) remarked:

> Recognising as we do that a comprehensively enjoyable campus environment is not just a physically attractive one, but one where no-one feels physically unsafe, or emotionally humiliated, the University Council and administration has continued to focus strongly on student and staff well-being, as the Vice-Chancellor will indicate in his address, including through the establishment of the Respectful Relationships Unit (State of the University Chancellor's Speech, 15 February 2019).

The remarks indirectly reference the appalling (indeed, the worst in the nation) results of the sexual violence survey, undertaken in 2017. The high rate of on-campus residency was blamed for the result, something that sits perhaps a little uncomfortably alongside the recent provision to students of the opportunity to live on campus on a scale far exceeding that of any of Australia's other major universities. Residential provision was indeed a key element of ANU's plan to become a small, but exclusive university in the style of Oxbridge (or Harvard); all students who wish to live on campus would be provided opportunity to do so. But accommodations set at a distance from central areas and tucked away into treed pockets are not just "fabulous" for students; they are also havens for predators—and nightmares to surveil. While the ANU fared worst of all—perhaps for the reasons cited above—the National Report on Sexual Assault and Sexual Harassment at University Campuses (Australian Human Rights Commission, 2017), indicated a lurking violence on campuses in general. The horrifying results showed the extent of sexual harassment and violence in university settings. Just over half of university students reported harassment on at least one occasion in 2016 and just under 7 percent of students experienced assault in 2015 or 2016. The relationship between "sexual assault and harassment" and "university campuses" was not lost on University of Melbourne's Maddie Spencer, who refused to see university spaces as simply the backdrop against which assaults occurred. Indeed, Spencer held campus environs partially responsible for assaults and harassments when she wrote up her analysis for Et Cetera, an online student magazine launched in 2019. Therein she remarked:

> I'm sure that on your walk through campus, it won't be too long before you find something named after a dead white man. A monument, plaque, room, lecture hall or building. Most of the time we don't pay that much attention to it, but subconsciously it could be having a greater impact on how we behave. Not only does it serve as a constant reminder to women that the odds are stacked against them (even more so for WOC and queer or trans people): it also reminds men of their power in these institutions, often founded in patriarchy. It reminds men that they are likelier to be celebrated and can give them an inflated sense of confidence. Without even noticing, we are being conditioned to recognise that men's achievements are more notable than women's.

Earlier in her piece, she noted that:

> The features of a space can influence our attitudes, our behaviours and how we interact with each other without us even recognising it. And no example is more relevant than our university campuses. A great example of this is the University of Melbourne's Parkville campus. While there is some effort to celebrate women (Elisabeth Murdoch, Alice Hoy), and new buildings are less commonly being named after people (such as Arts West and the Melbourne School of Design), there is still an abundance of facilities and monuments named after men. Now I'm sure that many of these people have made great accomplishments. I'm just not convinced that there's not that many women or people of colour who have done something equally noteworthy. "Power dynamics are really clear: when institutional buildings are named after men, when all the monuments are only about the achievements of men and the universities are indeed named after men, that communicates where the power lies," says Nicole Kalms. And you don't have to look far to see the consequences of this power imbalance. Change the Course cited numerous examples of misogyny in STEMM (Science, Technology, Engineering, Maths and Medicine) fields. Stories were detailed of lecturers not even bothering to learn their female students' names; a female PhD student being told that she only won an award because the judges wanted to sleep with her; and female students feeling that their achievements were continuously discredited against those of their male peers (Spencer, 2019).

Another uncomfortable violence lurking around and about the Kambri precinct development concerns the way in which the portmanteau of Oxford and Cambridge, the two oldest, wealthiest, and most famous universities in the United Kingdom, references not only academic excellence, but equally implies superior social or intellectual status or elitism. For some observers, the fact that the new Kambri precinct sits atop the former Union Square and drove some small businesses that could no longer afford the elevated rental costs out of campus trading altogether said it all (see for example Lindell, 2017). For some, a kind of class violence was afoot, and the university had come about as far from its intentions to be inclusive of "the public" as it was possible to go. It is, of course, much more complicated than the perspectives of irritated retailers might indicate; a public acknowledgment of Indigenous ownership of the land upon which Kambri sits, and the gifting of the word *Kambri* (loosely translated as "meeting place" from the local language[s] of the region), signals a belongingness on campus to Indigenous people that was not present in hear of the build environment before. We think this stands in some contrast to the argument we are about to make in respect to naming buildings after university women.

While examples such as these clearly indicate the entailment of physical campus restructure (and indeed all manipulations of space) with multiple potentialities for violence, we are particularly interested here in yet another, gendered, sort of violence that came to the fore in the process of naming the buildings included in the precinct.

As Sharon Bell remarked in 2009, women in the academy endure "differences in salary, *space,* awards, resources, and response to outside offers . . . despite professional accomplishments equal to those of their male colleagues" (2009: 442, our emphasis). Bell meant to refer to the peculiarities of dwelling in the university, such as differential allocation of spaces to men and women, and the male command of powerful institutional spaces. We attend in what follows to the ways in which campus buildings acquired the names of those ANU citizens considered worthy of memorialisation.

The institutional process of naming Kambri's new buildings included a public consultation phase. Everyone knew who the contenders were and knew that the decision had been taken to put forward only women candidates. Some of our interlocutors used the process to make assessments of the state of gender equity at the university; we feature two such women, and two memorialised women, below.

MARIE REAY AND HANNA NEUMANN
ARE NAMED HONORARY (WO)MEN?

In some very transparently put remarks, the university itself has had its own story to tell of the Kambri developments. Its official story provided a way to interpret how relations between self and built environs ought be understood, in and through the pursuit of gender and ethnic equity (see textbox 4.1). Such remarks certainly appear to make good intentions (literally) concrete. Buildings and their commitment to women (and Indigenous people) made and set in stone now and "forever" appear to be distinctive material stories that attest to the commitment of the institution to literally change the university's environment. But, as we will show over the course of this chapter, within this very declaration of transparent will to change lies the stern continuance of the male dominated past.

We want to note at the outset that the stories the institution tells provoke variously positioned recipients to respond. They might, variously, contest them, weave them into their sense of the institutional world, or reject them out of hand. Whatever response they provoke, stories enable people to operate on the relations between themselves and the other persons and things of the institutional world that constitute (multiple) reality(ies). The capacity of stories to invite such reworking permits no singularly asserted reality. Our informants Bette and Kirsten, who came from different disciplinary areas and who regarded the official ANU Kambri buildings story in almost opposite terms, each engaged interestedly with the ANU's official story. They each made the link between the institution and themselves in the political terms—made in the form of the pursuit of equity—on offer. Bette, for her part, rejected them out of hand.

"I'm pissed about it!," she exclaimed to Simone after reading the media release online. "Jesus Christ. It would be really radical if they named the teaching centre after a man, wouldn't it?" Bette explained that she was not trying to be disrespectful of the women who were to be memorialised in the new buildings, but she could see a pattern. "I think this [naming] makes an extension of the idea that women are good at nurturing students, doing the kind of pastoral care and guidance that men are considered less adept at," she said. "It's also at the very heart of the shopping and restaurant zone. The fluffy, social part—not the serious, academic part. I think that is probably of some significance." Bette was "a social scientist of gender, and a feminist"; "I know what it means," she said, grimly.

Where Bette "knew" that the building names articulated the pattern that is part of the naturalised gender discrimination of neoliberal patriarchy, and

THE WOMEN BEHIND KAMBRI'S BUILDINGS

JOPLIN LANE - Dr Germaine Joplin

Dr Germain Joplin was a Research Fellow in the Department of Geophysics from 1952 and an ANU Council member from 1969.

Her research into rock physics during the 1960s made a significant and enduring contribution to the field of geology.

"When I started in the early [19]20s girls were not supposed to go wandering about with maps and sacks of rocks, but if you were really interested in your work you had to . . . " *Germaine Joplin quoted in The Canberra Times, 6 August 1968, p. 10*

In 1982, she was awarded the W. R. Browne Medal for distinguished contributions to the Geological Sciences of Australia and became a Member of the Order of Australia (AM).

MARIE REAY TEACHING CENTRE - Dr Marie Reay

Dr Marie Reay was a pioneering ethnographer whose work was at the forefront of twentieth-century Australian anthropology.

Her research in the position of women in the PNG Highlands broke new ground, long before second-wave feminism brought interest in the position of women in society.

Dr Reay was a research fellow at the Research School of Pacific Studies from 1959 and an Advocate for Indigenous Australia, closely associated with Australian Institute of Aboriginal Studies.

Dr Marie Reay was an ANU Council member from 1969.

TANGNEY ROAD - Senator Dorothy Tangney

Senator Dorothy Tangney was the first woman member of the Australian Senate in 1943 and served on the first ANU Council from 1951 to 1968. During this time, she was the only woman on Council.

In her maiden speech to the Senate in 1943, she stressed her belief in women as equal partners in Australian society, and throughout her career made women's rights a high priority.

DI RIDDELL STUDENT CENTRE - Di Riddell

Di Riddell was the ANUSA Administrative Secretary from 1965 to 1990.

Riddell nurtured generations of students and was instrumental in establishing some of the key welfare and advisory services of ANUSA, as well as building support for the fledgling ANU Arts Centre (where she worked following her retirement from ANUSA in 1990).

She is remembered for her tireless work to support of the wide range of activists at ANU and as an important figure in the lives of students throughout her time at the Association.

CAROLINE LANE WALK - Caroline Lane

"Queen" Caroline Lane was a figure held in high esteem by both First Australians and non-Indigenous people in her lifetime.She is highly regarded and related to many of the contemporary Ngunawal and Ngambri families who are the traditional custodians of the land where Kambri is located.

Source: Australian National University (2019d).

that Ortner (1974) would perforce regard as the result of the classification of women into the category of "nature," Kirsten thought differently.

"Things are changing," declared Kirsten, who was about to retire from her associate professor role at the Australian National University. Her declaration was made on the basis of changes in university spaces. She explained,

I belong to a very male dominated part of the university in a STEM discipline and I have to say that for decades I've taken that dominance to represent the situation of women here as a whole. But I think I possibly have not been right about that, at least not for the entirety of the time I have been here. The fact that Kambri has such *female* presence means that a fundamental change has occurred here, and I think that because people at the very top have to be on board with sending a signal to women, and in fact it's more than that—they have to have come up with it. I don't think you can say it's tokenistic because it cost so much, it's right at the gateway to the university, and it will last forever. It's a serious thing to do with and for women.

It seems to us that both Bette and Kirsten were each engaged in correspondences with the built circumstances of the campus and with the only apparently straightforward remarks the university had made about them. The remarks and the buildings each entered a social and political interaction with Bette and Kirsten, making for rich and multiple exchanges between them. *Correspondences* is Tim Ingold's (2000, 2007, 2011) term to denote how interactions occur between buildings (or any things of the world) and persons. For Ingold, correspondence is a way of engaging with the world that differs from representation, which implies that buildings (for example) act only as billboards for meaning, flashing signals to us, at distance from us. In contrast, correspondences occur in the thick of material flows (and the sensory awareness of such flows) in experienced relationships between entities, like people and buildings. New things, or "fragments"—like new buildings, or decisions about their names, get caught up in the directionality and force of existing flows. Human agents do not wilfully control these flows; they are rather "immersed" in them. Things and persons encounter one another in the force of the flows and in this sense are involved in experimental relations with one another. Accordingly Ingold defines correspondence as seeing the state of things and sensing where they are going, in the thick of the flow. Both women could clearly see "where things were going" and, although their views very evidently differed, they shared the notion that a violence was being done or undone—Bette saw an old violence continuing, Kirsten saw an old violence coming, finally, to an end. But only one, Bette, saw a secret lurking in the good news story of naming buildings after prominent women.

Kambri is, as Bette said, located at the very heart of the campus, on the site formerly occupied by the Union building. That site is located very close to the new entrance to the institution, on University Avenue. Its location here certainly indicates, at first blush, a radical departure from a material manifestation of the patriarchy—and a heartening one for Kirsten as she prepared to depart an institution ostensibly much improved in gender equity terms from when she had entered it decades earlier.

Kambri opened to the public in early February 2019. The decision to name its two main buildings, the teaching building and the student centre, after Marie Reay and Di Riddell respectively was made under the ANU's Naming Policy. The policy includes several categories of naming; philanthropic naming, which recognises donor contributions; functional naming, which reflects the purpose or location of a building; and honorific naming, which recognises individuals who have made contributions to the institution, have lent their international reputation to the university, have brought disciplinary credit to it, or who have brought distinction to the institution resultant of their activities or particular reputation. The names given to the Kambri buildings (and surrounding streets) were made under the honorific category. The naming committee responsible for recommending names to the ANU Council includes the vice chancellor, who serves as chair; the chief operating officer, the deputy vice chancellor (academic) and/or deputy vice-chancellor (research) and/or deputy vice chancellor (global engagement); the deputy director (operations), alumni relations and philanthropy; the director of facilities and services; the director of corporate governance and risk; a college dean appointed by the vice chancellor, and one postgraduate or undergraduate student of the university.

Just prior to the time that names were being considered for the Kambri buildings, the then deputy vice chancellor (academic) Marnie Hughes-Warrington issued a public statement about how the existing names for buildings and streets on campus were "very white and male." Clearly aware of the idea that buildings could represent important sites for cultural meaning, social and political memory and public discourse, Hughes-Warrington wanted to correct the very clear gender imbalance in the naming of the physical spaces of the campus. Hers was a shared view and, eventually, it was made publicly known that all the names for the new buildings and streetscapes of Kambri would be, exclusively, female.

While naming buildings after clearly exemplary women is laudable and recognises female contributions in solid and enduring forms, the particular register in which they have been recognised leaves honorary legacies open to a number of interpretations—and, rather than conferring a sense of a future in which women figure more prominently, may in fact beget its opposite. There is a secret lurking in the transparent institutional remarks.

Of the forty-eight nonresidential buildings on the ANU campus, a total of five are named in honour of women who have made exceptional contributions to the ANU. The women are Beryl Rawson (1933–2010), Marie Reay (1922–2004), Di Riddell (1929–2019), Hanna Neumann (1914–1971) and Molly Huxley (?-1981). Of these, only one, the Hanna Neumann building, houses a research facility—the Mathematical Sciences Institute. The other four buildings house student services and teaching spaces.[2] The assignation of the named buildings to service and teaching functions, along with the paucity of buildings named after women, might itself be considered a physical manifestation of the patriarchy. Reay's case is particularly illustrative of this possibility.

An anthropologist, Reay spent twenty-nine years at the ANU. She is particularly renowned for her ethnographic work among the Kuma people in Papua New Guinea, and for her anthropological studies of Indigenous Australians. In 1953, Reay joined the department then called the Department of Anthropology and Sociology, having gained entrance via a research scholarship. Soon after her arrival, she departed with a group of academics dispatched to the Wahgi Valley in the largely unexplored Highlands of Papua New Guinea. She there distinguished herself as the first ethnographer to undertake a detailed investigation into the position of women in Highlands society.

Reay found herself in a male-dominated society in the Highlands but was herself treated by Kuma as an "honorary male," to the extent that she was privy to initiation rites for boys. Our colleague Francesca Merlan edited Reay's unfinished manuscript on her field research from the 1950s and 1960s on women's lives in the Wahgi Valley (Reay [Merlan] 2014). Reay's unfinished manuscript had been found in the course of mounting a 60th anniversary of Anthropology at the ANU, in 2011. Merlan found and reconstructed the work. The story Reay wanted to tell contrasted young girls' freedom in courting and selecting marriage partners with the restrictions and limitations they experienced after marriage. The work, with its introduction by eminent anthropologist of the Highlands, and of gender, Marilyn Strathern, is one centrally concerning gender relations, feminist anthropology and Melanesia. In 1965, when Reay wrote the manuscript, it was well ahead of its time. Had she published it then, it not only would have caused something of a feminist splash, rewriting as it does part of our understanding of gender relations in Melanesia; it would also have been the very first published ethnography of women's lives in the Central Highlands of Papua New Guinea.

Merlan notes in the work that Reay's field experiences and resulting findings stood in stark contrast with her institutional life:

> In contrast to her absorption in fieldwork, Reay's academic situations, and especially her appointment at The Australian National University, tried her, particularly in latter years. In his obituary, anthropologist Michael Young (2005: 83) remarks that Reay observed a succession of male departmental chairs and different styles of academic leadership. "As a graduate student she had been exploited by Elkin, bullied by Nadel, and patronized by Stanner, so she took a dim view of god-professors in general, and tended to remain aloof from departmental politics," he writes (ibid; see Reay 1992: 138–139). From personal acquaintance with Marie when I was at The Australian National University in 1981 as a visiting junior academic, and from conversations in the late 90s when I and my family visited her in her home on the central coast of New South Wales, I can attest that, at least for some of her working years, she felt persecuted under particular departmental chairmanship. She said that she was closely monitored by Professor and departmental head Derek Freeman, who often gave her up to ten directives and notes a day about her duties, and (at some point) denied her the right of supervising postgraduate students (though she clearly did supervise a number of students, including Pacific and New Guinean scholars Grant McCall, Daryl Feil, Wayne Warry and Epeli Hau'ofa).[13] She also, perhaps in conjunction with this, had some periods of mental instability and recurrent depression in later years. Reay remained bitter about the treatment meted out to her to the end of her life. . . . Was Reay a feminist in the sense of having a particular interest in women's lives, or liberation? Yes, in some ways. . . . In concluding this book Reay suggests that should women be treated more fairly and equally, and be enabled to have more control over their own lives—and she believes that this should happen—the society of the Minj Agamp as we know it would become unrecognisable, and its major structures would be significantly altered. While much change has occurred in the meantime, it is difficult to say that the social order has become radically altered or unrecognisable. Nor have women become "free" in the way Reay considered desirable. It is speculative, but all things considered, Reay may have shared some sense of oppression with them, especially in light of persecution she suffered in her academic situation (Reay [Merlan], 2014: xiv).

It is possible to run the line that the naming of a teaching building in honour of Reay, itself contained within an administrative services site, distinguishes her in the university not as honorary man, as she was among the Kuma, but as a model *woman* in the university—precisely that expectation from which she suffered, and precisely the category she most resisted. This may be read because her recognition is hitched to teaching, an activity often regarded of lesser value relative to research in the neoliberal university—despite the fact that its importance is publicly emphasised. Smith, Else and Crookes (2014) found that despite an institutional emphasis on teaching, its value stands distinctly at odds with the emphasis placed on the research agenda. Universities are more inclined to invest in emerging research areas that are of monetary value in the knowledge economy than they are to invest in teaching. In general, these are male and female dominated practices respectively, and so it is that an institution's prestige and economic values continue to be ensured by male participations (Smyth, 2017; see also Jones, 2013).

As we indicated in our second chapter, none of this is to say that teaching isn't lucrative, especially with respect of international students. It *is* to say, though, that in substantive terms, teaching is in many respects relatively undervalued compared with research. As May, Peetz and Strachan (2013) observe, a casualised labour force carries out a good deal of the teaching at Australian universities, where:

> 49 percent of all academic staff (on a headcount basis), and 53 per cent of all teaching and research academic staff (this excludes research only/research intensive academic staff) are employed on a casual basis (May et al., 2013: 258).

As they also observe, most of them are female. As Ortner (1974) would have said, teaching involves tending to the needs of others, a form of care related to a purportedly female capacity for nurturance (and a related lack of prestige, especially when the teaching is casualised and located at the very bottom of the institutional hierarchy—and pay scale). Also contributing to the lesser status of teaching is the difficulty of quantifying teaching quality. Certainly, students can assess its quality as part of student evaluations of learning and teaching, but this is a far cry from the comprehensive peer review rigour that is applied to research endeavours. There is some difficulty, then, in assessing teaching in the terms of value to the neoliberal institution. This is reflected perhaps most starkly in the fact that global university rankings are driven by research, not teaching, outcomes.

The result is that teaching (and service of many kinds) is practically absented from the measures by which academic outputs are valued in the knowledge economy (see for example Smith, Else & Crookes, 2014; Riddell, 2017).

The allocation of Reay to this arena, rather than to the research arena may, then, be telling. In contrast, Hanna Neumann might be considered to have been memorialised as an *honorary man*. ANU building number 145, located on Science Road, is named after the exemplary mathematician, who was born in Berlin in 1914. Neumann was an undergraduate at the University of Berlin, where she met the mathematician Bernhard Neumann, who would become her husband. Neumann began postgraduate research at the University of Gottingen in 1936. Her first years at university coincided with the ominous rise of the Nazi Party. Neumann developed a dangerous reputation with the party; she was among several who actively prevented the harassment of Jewish lecturers by preventing fascist sympathisers from gaining access to their lecture halls. Quickly, it became too dangerous for Neumann to remain in Germany and she fled in 1938 to join her fiancé, himself a Jewish refugee. Bernard Neumann had departed for England some years earlier. There, they married and had five children, and Hanna enrolled at Oxford University to complete her doctoral research, from which she graduated DPhil in 1944. In 1955, she was awarded one of Oxford's Higher Doctorates, Doctor of Science (DSc.), an award that recognises excellence in academic scholarship. She held academic positions in the UK at Hull and Manchester, and then, in 1963, she and her husband were given posts at the ANU, where Hanna was made Professor and Head of the Department of Pure Mathematics from 1964 to 1971, and Dean of Students from 1968 to 1969. This made Hanna the first woman to be appointed to a Chair at the Australian National University, and the first female professor of mathematics in Australia.

It was no mean feat. Besides a career shaped in part by the rise of Nazism, Hanna entered a university environment of deep patriarchal sentiment and practice. In 1957, just a few years before Hanna took up her post, Sir Keith Hancock, head of the Research School of Social Sciences at ANU, had written the then Vice Chancellor Sir Leslie Melville to communicate his thoughts on appointing academic women, indicating the general sharedness of his view. He reportedly remarked in a jovial tone, "it is no private fad of my own to insist that good professors will not long continue to do their best work unless they are reinforced by charwomen."[3] Neumann had risen beyond her station to a position of success, in a profoundly male-dominated discipline—and she is recognised precisely as such in the material legacy that is ANU Building 145, named in her honour in 1973. Neumann's legacy is equivalent to the ways in which men are memorialised in the university's built environs; in the terms of research, not in the terms of teaching, or service. Reay's is not. Perhaps then, the fact that a building is named after a woman is insufficient for indicating the demise of the patriarchy, as Bette "knew"; this is at least as possible as the idea that building names indicate that gender equity is achieved, something of which Kirsten felt assured.

Our sense is that Athena is, so to speak, the ANU built campus. She appears, as she often did in the Homerian classic, in a form other than her own to accomplish Odysseus's command, namely for the ward to *"grow in wisdom without rebellion"*(Anderson and Shannon, 1995: 25–26, our emphasis). On the basis of the university's transparent remarks, we may acquire the agreeable wisdom, that the accomplishments of women must be recognised in enduring forms by the institution to ensure their memorialisation and future inclusion. In the case of Reay, the memorialisation is accurate; the building named in her honour continues, in a way, the institutional repression she suffered in her institutional lifetime, in that the building constrains and refuses her due place in the research pantheon. It instead allocates her as a woman in a patriarchal system, as she experienced in her own lifetime. The terms of inclusion ensure that no rebellion against the patriarchy can occur. It may be that women are memorialised in the very terms by which they are excluded from full participation in the modern university, ensuring an historical continuance of the diminished institutional status of women. Athena is also present, doing hers and the Mentor's job of ensuring wisdom without rebellion in other ways in institutional context. Neumann is something of an exception. The rarity of the form, though, very effectively makes the case that the patriarchy is very much practically present in the built environs of the campus. In the example we discuss below, Athena again appears, but in something closer to her own form—in the inclusion of the Athena SWAN program at the ANU.

ATHENA'S SWAN SONG

Another very transparent remark is made by the university in respect to gender equity, or, rather, the lack of it. This one comes in the form of the inclusion of the Athena SWAN program, which the ANU has recently joined. Athena SWAN (Scientific Women's Academic Network) is a charter established and managed by the UK Equality Challenge Unit (now part of Advance HE) in 2005. It purposefully bears the name of the Goddess, ostensibly to recognise Athena's association with skill, wisdom, counsel and mentoring and thus with the emancipation of women from the dominance of men. Perhaps it also has to do with Athena's association with war and her skill in ensuring battleground victories. But Athena was also the guardian of the welfare of kings. The program named after her, we suggest, also (and most ironically) protects dominant male interests.

The Athena SWAN program recognises and rewards the institutional advancement of gender equality. Its founding charter set out to support and recognise institutional commitments to advancing the careers of women in science, technology, engineering, mathematics, and medicine (STEMM).

GENDER EQUITY & INCLUSION

ANU is committed to equity and diversity, and is actively building a more inclusive culture where all staff are supported to reach their full potential in their academic or professional careers. Over recent years the University has made some progress on gender equity, however we recognise that there is more to be done.

There is still a high gender imbalance amongst academic staff, with around twice as many men as women. About half of the University's PhD graduates are women, but just one quarter of senior academics at ANU are women.

The loss of so many women from the career pipeline is a waste of talent, and negatively impacts our capacity for world-class research and innovation.

In 2016, ANU became an inaugural member of the SAGE Pilot of Athena SWAN in Australia. Athena SWAN is a UK-based evaluation and accreditation program that recognises excellence in employment practices that promote gender equity and inclusion. Since its establishment in the UK in 2005, Athena SWAN has proven to be a powerful framework that has helped to improve gender diversity and strengthen women's leadership roles within participating institutions in the UK.

While the focus of SAGE is on the STEMM disciplines, ANU has chosen to examine gender equity and diversity issues in the context of the entire University, including the Humanities and Social Science disciplines and Professional staff.

As a member of SAGE, ANU is currently working towards Bronze institutional accreditation. The project is currently in a data collection and analysis phase, with a four year action plan to be developed later in 2018. The University's application for a Bronze Athena SWAN institutional award is due 31 March 2019.

As part of our commitment to equity and diversity, ANU is determined to create better outcomes for women through the improvement of hiring, promotion and retention of women, while creating a more inclusive work environment for everyone.

Source: Australian National University (2019a).

In May 2015 the charter was expanded to include non-STEMM departments including arts, humanities, social sciences, business, and law. This expansion was accompanied by the inclusion of professional, support and technical staff, and students. The inaugural non-STEMM award was made in 2016.

The awards have clout; in 2011, the UK Chief Medical Officer made it a requirement for academic departments applying for funding from the English National Institution of Health Research to hold the Athena SWAN silver award.[4] The ANU presently aspires to hold the (foundational) Bronze Award, as it says in its official remark (see textbox 4.2 above). It aspires to achieve this award because, as it also says, gender equity has not been achieved at the university.

The inclusion of Athena SWAN as an antidote to gender inequity interests us greatly—and not only because it requires the inclusion of named mentoring programs. Ostensibly, the university's achievement against gender equity goals is decided by the process of external accreditation and held accountable to an internationally recognised Gold (or in this case, Bronze) standard.

Developed in 2005 by Advance HE, a UK-based not-for-profit that supports strategic change and continuous improvement in higher education, Athena SWAN began as the Athena project. The Athena Project operated between 1999 and 2007, when it merged with the Scientific Women's Academic Network (SWAN), to advance the representation of women in STEMM disciplines. In May 2015, the arts, humanities, social sciences, business and law (AHSSBL) were added, as were professional and support roles. In the same year, a foundational concern with gender expanded to include transgender staff and students, as well as others affected by insufficiently recognised barriers to advancement in the institution. At the basis of the founding Charter are ten areas that institutions commit to progress, including unequal gender representation, gender pay disparity, ensuring active leadership from senior staff (including the establishment of mentoring programs). Self-assessment against the areas from all institutional staff levels can result in accreditation, beginning at the Bronze level. Attainment at higher levels requires institutions to commit to ongoing culture change, and to make concrete plans for their achievement. As Wilkinson (2019) notes, this requires a very large amount and range of data, including:

> data on students; application processes, attainment, and student destination after graduating; data on staff, including progression and promotional data, uptake of training, awareness and use of flexible working, and leave policies, amongst many other things. This range of data is a significant burden to collect, often involving multiple sources across the institution. . . . Beyond this data, Athena SWAN involves collecting the views and perspectives of staff and students . . . that includes surveys of undergraduates, postgraduate research students, and staff, as well as professional and technical teams, and focus groups to gather qualitative insights . . . each Athena SWAN application and award is supported by a self-assessment team, including staff working at a range of grades, in professional, technical and academic roles. It also includes student

representation. . . . The self-assessment team aims to be representative of a range of working and personal contexts, including male representation and support.

Remarking on her own institution's attainment of the Bronze level, Wilkinson notes that Athena SWAN,

> is not about inactivity once an award has been achieved; instead each department or institution will have produced a significant action plan, on which they must demonstrate and evidence progress over the coming years. These actions are encouraged to be "SMART" (specific, measurable, attainable, realistic and timely), with named individuals associated to actions, and identifying the priorities to be tackled with the greatest urgency. . . . Our application and action plan are circulated to the whole department, adding transparency and ownership to actions for the future.

No wonder, then, that our informant, thirty-two-year-old STEMM discipline member Andrea, was tired. She said she was "Busy!! Always too busy"—in her substantive position as senior lecturer and in her role as part of the Athena SWAN self-assessment team for an Australian university that had already scored itself a Bronze Institutional Award. In Australia, there are forty-five institutions participating in the Science in Australia Gender Equity (SAGE) process. Andrea was a named member on one of these forty-five institutional teams, and, Andrea said,

> like the majority of them as far as I know, the one I'm on is all-female. We're responsible for putting together the next stage of my institution's bid for Silver.

Remarking on her institution's attempts to attract male staff members to the self-assessment team, she said: "They tried. But no takers. I understand why—it's shit tonnes of work."

We are interested primarily in the inclusion of the Athena SWAN program in the ANU's gender equity strategy for the way in which it mirrors what we argue mentoring programs themselves do: *ironically, they imitate the structures they seek to change.* This is a secret kept right in the thick of the university's transparency: the announcement of inclusion in a rigorous and purpose built gender program for the purpose of setting right the lamentable problem of gender inequity is unassailable. But, as Tzanakou and Pearce (2019: 3) argue, institutional participation in the program very typically leads to additional, unpaid labour *for the very women that are meant to be emancipated by the program.* The rosy transparency garners capital for the institution, even as women are thrust deeper into the conditions the program is meant to alleviate.

Rosser, Barnard, Carnes and Munir (2019) note, for example, that the required self-assessment teams are, more often than not, majority populated by, and almost exclusively led by, women. Rosser et al. also note that this labour is not generally reflected in workloads; MacFarlane (2018) describes how such labour constitutes yet more unrecognised "housework" for female staff. Andrea felt it keenly, in her "overwhelming exhaustion, lack of time for being with my kids, and in general always feeling shit-scared of not publishing fucking anything this year." Andrea's "neck hurt constantly," and she felt her "eyes and back" strain and suffer because of the long hours she had to put in on multiple work fronts. Andrea did not complain, "except like right now, to you," because doing Athena's work was important and worthwhile, even if you never saw your kids, or got any other work done. The secret is thus preserved: the transparent dedication of the university to such important work made it all the more important to do—despite the obvious ironies involved. The feminised patterning of labour was writ deep into Andrea's body as she played her part in the achievement of gender equity goals. Its silence, made in her decision not to sully the unassailable reputation of the program's titular Goddess and the work carried out in her name meant that the unnamed institution's commitment to Anthena SWAN could not be read as anything other than precisely a commitment to bringing about gender equity for all its staff, even as participation in it further entrenched unpaid and unrecognised feminine labour, and allocated the "housekeeping" duties of the institution to the members most suited to such domestic drudgery.

While the counter narratives that threatened to reveal Athena SWAN as an Ugly Duckling remained largely expressed by dedicated Andreas in silent soma—in their necks bent sore from doing data entry too long, in eyes dry and strained, they were sometimes loudly and baldly proclaimed.

DISPUTING TRANSPARENT CLAIMS
AND THE RISE OF BETWIXTNESS

We have suggested so far that institutions might see value in candidly reporting dire states of gendered play. When they do, they might accrue transparency capital, irrespective of what the result of the declaration is—no change in the male-dominated built campus, yet more enslavement of women in the drudgery of housekeeping work, as in the case of Athena SWAN. We want to suggest in this part of our chapter that disputing transparent institutional stories of gender equity articulates that something else might happen besides the institutionally claimed advancement in gender relations. Disputations are also central to women's senses of the status of the patriarchy. Perhaps surprisingly, disputations of official stories and statements did not result in women sighing and resigning themselves to the ever-endurance of male dominance. They were much more often—at least for our informants—indicative of the state of the patriarchy, between thriving and unassailable and dead in the water.

Stories of the ideally diminishing patriarchy might appear as compulsory reporting on gender participation. They might appear as rankings issued by the *Times Higher Education World University Rankings* that in 2019 commenced effectively admonishing or praising universities by ranking them in order of diminishing success on their efforts to close the gender gap in pay, position and activity divisions between education, research and service for men and women (see Times Higher Education, 2019). These and institutionally developed stories could also be set against stories that were *not* told—literally, in the case of thirty-five-year-old social scientist Kylie. She couldn't find the ANU listed on the *Times Higher Education* gender rankings. She had also seen the ANU Gender Equity page we reproduced earlier in this chapter describing the university's entrance into the Anthea SWAN program. Kylie described the page and its contents as "a nice, warm, fuzzy, feel-good story" that showed the university was doing "fuck all." She made the remark in relation to the fact that if one clicked on ANU's Gender Equity & Inclusion news page, the most recent story to be found there was from January 2019, some eleven months before we interviewed her (this remains the case at the time of writing, in 2022). ANU has in fact since been awarded the Bronze Athena Swan accreditation (conferred in September 2019—see Australian National University 2019a), but to Kylie, the fact that the gender equity news page remained outdated was a far better indicator of where the institution actually stood on gender. She was annoyed that to be found on the Newsroom page announcing the accreditation was a line saying: "SAGE Athena SWAN is not a box-ticking exercise. Since committing to the pilot in 2016 the University has launched a range of initiatives to support and advance the careers of women and men." "But they can't keep up a Gender Equity news page, though, can they? What does that say? To me it says BOX TICKING EXERCISE! Because wouldn't there be stuff on there if Athena SWAN actually translated into stuff that could actually be reported there?"

Since we interviewed Kylie in 2019, the ANU became the first international base for Global Institute for Women's Leadership (GIWL), in 2020. GIWL ANU works in partnership with GIWL at King's College London, focussing on the Asia-Pacific region—and it specifically acknowledges the depressingly glacial rate of progress insofar as closing the global gender gap is concerned—over ninety-nine years, according to the World Economic Forum. That very transparent disclosure both, we think, stitches together transparency and secrecy in interdependence; the university can do something tangible, real, to address the gender gap at the very same moment as it, along with other organisations according to the World Economic Forum, operates almost a century behind gender equity. There's no secret in that story, as we noted in our third chapter.

For Kylie, "real" stories detailing on the ground experience had trumped another kind of story, and so the institution had contradicted itself, accidentally revealed the truth of the matter and in so doing revealed where Kylie herself stood relationally to the patriarchy. She didn't matter. But she also knew that if the university was publicly declaring itself dedicated to gender levelling projects, she would be able to ask for things, and get them. "I'll be laying the whole 'I need support because I'm a woman' thing on pretty thickly, too," she cackled:

> It's a good line to go with when you need something, and one that men can't take away. In that sense, the university saying it is dedicated to enhancing the status of women does indeed work—but it puts it all on you [on women] to do all the work. You have to play the lady card, and I have actually been accused of doing that before—by a colleague. So rude. He acted like things were perfectly even in the first place. Just all jealousy—he can't say things like, "I need this conference money because presenting in this field which is underrepresented by women will enhance the status of women in that field." When you're in a situation of inequity, you play the hand you are dealt.

Other kinds of stories might be set against one another, to devastating effect on glossy "historical landmark" claims, such as those made by Frank Larkins in 2018, which declared that women had achieved slightly higher institutional participation than men. It was all well and good to produce a set of statistics that revealed an increase in hiring women remarked "forty-ish" Tamara, who wanted to be identified only as working in "a STEMM discipline" in an Australian university that had announced that particular accomplishment at a morning tea celebrating International Women's Day a few years ago. But how, wondered Tamara, could the university possibly regard itself as improved on the gender equity question when women still could not break into the professoriate, according to statistics on the Australian Research Council website? It did not help, she reckoned, that a senior female member of the professoriate—a person already rarely and safely ensconced there—delivered the statistical gains to a group of assembled women who were not, and who might not ever be, according to the ARC statistics, professors. On the one hand, the person announcing this good news story was, in fact, a woman. On the other hand, the statistics, according to Tamara, were, evidently, "fucked."

Disputations and praises of such stories of the greater or lesser inclusion of women, burnish them with different finishes as they are handled and reworked by interested parties. We ourselves as members of a research university and researchers of this topic engaged with the stories, troubling the partial presentations data we detected in Larkins's report. We placed the story instead within the story we knew was of most value to our own institution: the (most) valuable story of research, just as we had done with respect to buildings and their naming. The result is that one cannot claim the precise position of the patriarchy. It is certainly declared to be on the way out in institutional claims—but those same claims obscure the probability of its ongoing operation. Kylie, Tamara, Bette and Kirsten's interpretations of institutional stories furnished them with indications of the state of the patriarchy, but in the end no sure fix on whether it was possible. Even though Bette knew the buildings being named after women were named within a certain kind of patriarchal convention, they were still named after women, and were named in the centre of the campus. Kirsten set her knowledge, gained on the eve of her exit from the institution, in the context of a career; she was "perhaps wrong" in her sense of how it was, after all. Tamara could see before her, at morning tea, those women whom ARC statistics indicated were rarities; but perhaps in the future—her aspirational future—they would not be. As she held institutional stories to the account of their absences, Kylie left open the possibility that they might yet be filled with "real" stories that would prove the Athena SWAN accreditation more than a box-ticking exercise. For almost all of our informants, "the patriarchy" was located between the poles of dead and alive; now and then; nobody quite knew in what form and when it would emerge. It was in many respects "historical," but never to the extent that it could be consigned to a period, for it remained a living legacy and made its presence felt in the future. This was abundantly evident in statistical reporting that tracked the progress that had been made to bring about its death, declared often to be imminent in numbers demonstrating the reduction of gender equity gaps in pay and A, B, C academic levels, yet it lay in wait in the future for those aspiring to become part of the professoriate in predictions of how many years it would take for women to enjoy the same access to levels D and E as men presently do, as Tamara wondered.

For some women we interviewed, its location betwixt life and death lent "the patriarchy" a specific, useful, deployable spectral quality; it could be strategically deployed to greatest effect because it had been effectively killed, yet it lived on. That meant it could appear as a ghost that possessed particularly terrifying properties that could be wielded against men, should circumstances call for it. "So much has been achieved, we've come such a long way," declared forty-eight-year-old Teena, who didn't want to say which discipline she specialised in, or give her academic level—we only know she worked at a large UK university that she preferred we did not name:

> But that means it's an effective weapon now, because there's so much awareness of how bad universities have been to, and for, women. That means the very

invocation of the term has a really profound effect on men, especially senior men who were the perpetrators of the worst injustices. All you have to do is mention that what they are doing or saying might be patriarchal and there's an immediate and actually sometimes quite hilarious effect. It's like you've banged them on the head with a club in a silent movie. They go all cross eyed and back-track and explain that wasn't what they meant at all.

Teena was very careful to explain that her capacity and willingness to wield "the patriarchy" as a weapon was not disrespectful as she feared it might appear, because "when I have to say to someone that they are being sexist, they are! It's just that now it is recognised as a weapon, but women can pick it up and use it back." The chiasmusical character—critically, not a character of inversion but of betwixtness—permits the patriarchy's dual parts—its life and its death, its history and its unknown future—to be balanced, by the reversal of their structures.

The lively quality of the patriarchy was experienced differently by fifty-two-year-old Juliet, who was also a (mid-career) member of a STEMM discipline in the US. She had internalised the story her own mentor, now deceased, had told her many years earlier: that being a woman in the institution meant "double trouble." Double trouble meant one could expect double the trouble if a foot was put wrong—that could mean anything, from inappropriate tears when a publication rejection letter arrived to prosecuting a supervisory role too meekly or too harshly, or in other words being too much like a woman, or overcompensating and being too much like a man while still being a woman. Striking the right performative note was difficult and certainly double the trouble as for a man, but the real doubling came in terms of productivity. Women, claimed Juliet's mentor, had to be twice as good as men to be regarded as half their worth, "especially in the sciences," and that meant producing twice as many research outcomes in high quality outlets. Juliet certainly felt it menacing her as it meant she could "never rest to enjoy my success, and have always felt like what I do and how much I do is enough, or good enough," but it also motivated her to be,

> the most productive researcher in my department, even though I also teach, and in some cases I teach more than my male counterparts. I am very proud of my research record.

For Juliet, we might say that "the patriarchy" felt somewhere between something that pursued her, always there nipping at her heels, and something she pursued herself, as she sought to be as good as—and better than—the men who belonged to it.[5]

However promulgated, and irrespective of the regard in which they are held, stories of the patriarchy dwell between poles. Here, they acquire all the unruliness and unboundedness of anything liminally located. They stand as stories without ending, unresolved; they tell of institutions that claim to undo patriarchal systems and structures, as much as they indicate that gender equity has not as yet been achieved. Patriarchal structures stand at the threshold, between their not-quite-yet previous ways of structuring gendered identities, communities, outputs, roles, progressions, modes of governance and administrative functions, and a new, striven-for structuring that mentoring, ostensibly at least, aims to usher into being. This of course can happen only when a new state has been firmly established and can be publicly declared to a community who accepts that it is so. Until then, continuity of tradition becomes uncertain, future outcomes once taken for granted are thrown into uncertainty, and an awaiting of that which is to come pervades as new institutions, customs, practices, ideas, rules, arrangements, understandings, structures and feelings swell in readiness for establishment as the new official order of things.

Such ideas belong to the anthropological canon, and specifically to van Gennep (1960) and Turner (1969). Noting that liminality is regarded as a time of withdrawal from normal modes of social action, Turner spoke to the ways in which people could scrutinise the foundational values and axioms of the culture (1969: 156). Liminality must eventually resolve into a state; either the individual returns to the surrounding social structure, or else liminal communities develop their own internal social structure, or normative *communitas*.

The philosopher Karl Jaspers (1949 [2011]) was more interested in the application of such concepts to the collapses of order experienced by whole societies and institutions. His conceptualisation of the "the axial age" describes a period betwixt two structured world views and between two periods of empire building. These are creative periods in which "man [sic] asked radical questions," and where the "unquestioned grasp on life is loosened" ([1949] 2011: 2; see also Jaspers, 2003: 98).

Although the difference between the anthropological and philosophical versions might seem simply scalar (and of course historical) two distinctions extremely pertinent to our exploration of mentoring must be made. The first concerns the temporally contained points of entry to and exit from the liminal period itself; the second concerns the role of the "ceremony masters" who guide and shepherd those leaving one state and entering another.

One primary characteristic of liminality, as is evident in Turner's formulation, is that there is a way in as well as a way out; in ritual passages, members of the society are themselves aware of the liminal state: they know that they will leave it sooner or later, and will have "ceremony masters" to guide them through the rituals. In liminal periods that occur on a societal or institutional scale, the future beyond the liminal period remains largely unknown; while there might be plans, desires, strategic visions and indicators that attempt to illuminate, forecast and reel in this future, and while there are swellings and readyings of feelings and processes that wait for their day, the day itself is uncertain.[6]

PATRIARCHY STORIES IN AN AXIAL AGE

The second of Jaspers's points gives us leave to specifically consider mentoring within the not-quite-established-not-quite-disestablished patriarchy. This second point relates to the fact that in periods of wholesale change affecting an entire society (or in our case, an institution) there are no "ceremony masters," no learned leaders, who have gone through the process before and can, therefore, lead people out of it to a sure and certain destination. As Jaspers notes, it is here that liminal situations become dangerous because they allow for the emergence of self-proclaimed ceremony masters who assume leadership positions and wind up perpetuating liminality. They do so, intentionally or not, by emptying the liminal moment of real, authentic creativity, and turn it instead into the work of mimetic rivalry.

The same processes of mimetic rivalry plague current mentoring programs that have their genesis in ousting patriarchal orders. In our next chapter, we explore how named mentoring programs do precisely this.

NOTES

1. *Kambri* means "Meeting Place" for the ACT's Traditional Owners, who gifted the name to the university in 2018 (see Roberts, 2018).

2. The Beryl Rawson Building houses the College of Arts and Social Sciences student lounge, and offices for the College, including the offices of the Dean and Associate Deans and General Manager. Rawson began her work at the ANU in 1964. Over the thirty-four years of her ANU career, which saw her retire Professor Emerita, Rawson elevated the status of Classical Studies at the university and was elected Dean of Arts, in 1981. After two terms in the role, Rawson became Chair of the Department of Classics in 1989, a role she held until her compulsory retirement in 1998 at age sixty-five. Interestingly, despite the fact that Rawson was one of the very few women to occupy a senior executive position, she was unconcerned with gender discrimination. Deeply concerned with the Dawkins reforms, she remarked in an interview for a Faculty Oral History Program that they would result in a loss of crucial collegiality among academics, who would be "too busy" with the new bureaucracy to develop new ideas in collectivity.

Di Riddell Student Centre houses the ANU Student Association (ANUSA), the Postgraduate and Research Students Association (PARSA) and a number of student

services functions. ANUSA and PARSA, along with a number of other student services. Riddell entered the university through the Student Association in 1964, when
she was asked to fill in for an absent staff member. The few weeks' work turned into
a thirty year career, during which she was deeply involved in organising activism
efforts for the promotion of women's and Indigenous rights. Riddell served as the
Administrative Secretary of ANUSA from 1965 to 1990, and then as manager of the
ANU Arts Centre from 1990 until her compulsory retirement in 1995. Because of
the contract under which she worked, Riddell was not entitled to any superannuation
when she retired.

The Molly Huxley Building is the gatehouse at the entrance of University House.
The wife of Vice Chancellor Leonard Huxley, who served from 1960 to 1967, Molly
Huxley was the first lecturer in British History at the ANU. In 1961, she founded the
ANU Club for Women, which wound up in 2018. The Club was founded in response
to the ANU merger with the Melbourne University–affiliated Canberra University
College, which resulted in a significant influx of new staff and visitors to campus. The
CFW provided support for newly arrived female staff and female spouses.

3. Quoted in Grimshaw and Francis (2014: 212).

4. Evidence of achievement is, increasingly, important for institutions to retain
the right to apply for funding to research councils, which might require organisations to demonstrate that they meet policies on equality, diversity and inclusion. This
is presently the case in the UK, for instance; since 2011, the National Institute for
Health Research (NIHR) has required Athena SWAN accreditation for some funding
schemes.

5. For philosophical theoreticians like Kate Manne (2017) the patriarchy must be
considered in terms of its duality, but her terms are different from the betwixtness we
have described in the foregoing. A key moment arose for Manne's analytic parsing of
the patriarchy on the occasion of former Australian Prime Minister Julia Gillard's now
infamous Misogyny Speech. The 2012 speech was a parliamentary speech delivered
by Australian Prime Minister Julia Gillard on 9 October 2012, in reaction to alleged
sexism from the opposition leader Tony Abbott. It was preceded by some acute gendered attacks on the then Prime Minister; prior to it, Gillard had been the recipient of
remarks including those made by Bill Heffernan, Liberal Party member of the Senate representing the state of New South Wales from September 1996 to May 2016.
The often controversial and outspoken Heffernan remarked that the unmarried and
childless Gillard was "unfit for leadership because she was deliberately barren" (The
Bulletin, 2007). Other similarly derogatory comments came from politicians and jour-
nalists alike about her personal life and its effect on her Prime Ministership. Perhaps
the most offensive of the attacks came on the occasion of a (Liberal-National Party)
Coalition fundraiser that included a satirical menu with a dish named "Julia Gillard
Kentucky Fried Quail—Small Breasts, Huge Thighs & a Big Red Box." As Manne
(2017) has noted, Gillard's resultant speech served to clarify that misogyny and
sexism are distinct concepts, designating two branches of patriarchy. While sexism
serves to rationalize and justify the patriarchal order, misogyny polices and enforces
it. Manne argues that "sexism is an ideology that supports patriarchal social relations"
(5). Sexism accepts and undergirds gender roles with a foundational naturalising,

making them appear as outgrowths of a natural order so unassailable they appear as givens, or the natural order of things (see also Ortner, 1974 who conceptualises this in different terms with a similar practical result). In this sense, sexism is a belief system. Misogyny upholds this system; it is defined by Manne as an effort to control and punish women "who challenge male dominance" (5). For Manne, misogyny is not centrally defined by male hostility towards or hatred of women; rather it is "the law enforcement branch of the patriarchy . . . it is a way women are kept in [patriarchal] order, by imposing social costs for those breaking role or rank, and warning others not to" (5–6). As the enforcement "arm" of the patriarchy, misogyny does not require any particular sexist attitudes of enforcers. That distinction provides a productive gap that permits the continued oppression of women without overtly aggressive sexism.

6. This is not least, in the case of the patriarchy, because of its rhizomic quality, meaning that one of its parts might be forcefully removed—such as when a gender discrimination policy is installed that expressly outlaws bias—the patriarchy yet lives in the bulk of the buildings that are named after men. Despite the naming of new buildings in honour of women that we mentioned earlier, for example, material legacies refuse to be consigned to the past because they are material memories that both, and simultaneously, acquire and emit multiple (and often contradictory) meanings. Not the least of these meanings is the prestige that clings to and offgasses from buildings named after men—often those that house the most prestigious of the university's disciplines. Institutional mastery over stories about the patriarchy was not achieved—nor was a mastery of counterstory, as reflected in the myriad opinions and feelings expressed by women (including ourselves) who variously accepted and rejected them. The variances led us to closely consider the openness of the future that always dogs the change from one distinctive period to another.

Chapter 5

Payback Does Not *Appear* to Be a Bitch[1] (but It Is)

ATHENA'S ORIENTATION

In this chapter, Athena appears as Mentor, just as she often did in the Homerian classic, inhabiting his body to provide wisdom to the young ward. We argue herein that the women-only practice we examined mimics the patriarchal forms it abhors, as junior women are formed into male replicants—a form their mentors have already acquired. In pursuing these lines of inquiry, our chapter makes contemporary sense of Athena's appearance in the classic tale as the male Mentor.

In this chapter, we make the debt relations of mentoring plain, arguing that their generous calibre masks hierarchical relations not at all dissimilar from those operational between men and women of the institution. We closely examine a host of rules that apply to mentoring to reveal that generosity is not a unidirectional outpouring of resources from mentors to mentees, but instead a complex exchange relationship based on debt.

We reveal generous relations as a form of virtuous generosity, which begets hierarchical arrangement; we contrast these against a corporeal generosity that values difference—and we speculate as to whether such a form might arise in the university in the wake of COVID-19, a possibility we continue in the conclusion of this work.

GENEROSITY

Generosity has been a mainstay of anthropological exploration. The first half of Mauss's *The Gift: The Form and Reason for Exchange in Archaic*

Societies (1925) is dedicated to generosity (and, in fact, greed) and the obligation to reciprocate. For Mauss, gifts are not free; they bring about reciprocal exchange. Asking, "what power resides in the object given that causes its recipient to pay it back?," Mauss answers, the gift is a "total prestation" imbued with "spiritual mechanisms." Givers do not simply give in the material domain—they give part of themselves: "the objects are never completely separated from the men [sic] who exchange them" (1925:31). The divisions between spiritual and material domains thus "almost magically" transcended, the act of giving creates a social bond with an obligation to reciprocate on the part of the recipient. Not to reciprocate means to lose honour and status, but the spiritual implications can be even worse.

As David Graeber (2000) has noted, at the heart of Mauss's inquiry was the dismissal of the mythical society based on barter. Instead, objects circulated as gifts and

> almost everything we would call "economic" behavior was based on a pretense of pure generosity and a refusal to calculate exactly who had given what to whom. Such "gift economies" could on occasion become highly competitive, but when they did it was in exactly the opposite way from our own: Instead of vying to see who could accumulate the most, the winners were the ones who managed to give the most away (2000: np).

Equally central was the dismissal of the idea that such systems were alien and opposite to our own (Western) systems. Anyone who has ever received a gift knows well the obligation to repay it. Anyone who has ever given or received in unequal measure knows all too well the lingering, haunting discomfiture of inadequate reciprocity. Graeber was of a mind to declare such experiences "examples of universal human feelings, which are somehow discounted in our own society but in others were the very basis of the economic system" (2000: np). The difference, as Gregory (1982) explains, is inalienability. In a commodity economy objects and persons are rendered distinct in and through the conception of private property so that ownership rights over objects are fully transferred on their sale and thus alienated from the original owner. In a gift economy they remain unalienated from their givers. Thus, the identity of the giver remains inextricably intertwined with the object, and it is this that imbues the gift with the power to compel the recipient to reciprocate. Because gifts are inalienable they must be returned, otherwise there remains a debt that can only be repaid on reciprocation. In this way, a relationship is created between the giver and the receiver.

Such ideas as these problematize the notion of the free gift. Indeed, it is difficult to think of an occasion upon which a gift is given with no expectation of return, and that does not, in the creation of obligatory reciprocity, call forth and maintain a relationship between the giving and receiving parties. It is something of a standing anthropological challenge to come up with a contradicting example. A still-circulating (if that pun can be forgiven) possibility concerns blood donation: a debate extending from the mid-1970s, when Titmuss (1970) first explored it, until the present time. It is clear that blood donors (like givers to charity) have conferred upon them the prestige of being generously inclined, and perhaps even an expectation that generosity would at one time be repaid in receipt of same in the future; blood donors may contribute to the pool (another dreadful pun) so that they might one day receive it back in their own time of need. These are perhaps enough to render the gift of blood one that will eventually be returned to the giver. But the question remains as to whether a social relationship is created in the act of giving it. This question is complexified in the case of blood and of organ donation, where anonymity insures recipients against the dreadful affective and symbolic burdens of receiving and having to reciprocate the gift of life. The paradox, as Steiner (2003) notes, "is that this makes it hard for us to see such giving as a social tie, whereas that value—the affective and symbolic value of a social tie—has generally been the one associated with this form of commerce between human beings" (2003: 162).

Blood and its sociality notwithstanding, mentoring could certainly be understood in the gift exchange terms Mauss sets out. Indeed, several works have specifically interrogated mentoring in precisely these terms (see for example Kamvounias, McGrath-Champ & Yip, 2008; Clouder & Adefila, 2014; Dobbins & Fell, 2019). In general, these works have set out to illuminate the dyadic relationship between mentor and mentee so as to correct the view that mentoring is an outpouring of one-way altruistic generosity that is received by passive mentees who bear no obligation of reciprocity. We begin our exploration of mentoring as gift exchange by, first, examining generosity.

GENEROUS EXCHANGES

Mentoring is generally considered a generous act. It might be understood as the index of a willingness to work with those less equipped, less experienced; to give of one's precious time that might otherwise have been elsewhere invested. Giving certainly occurs in mentoring practice: the abundant magnanimity of mentors is, as the following excerpts indicate, recognised by mentors and mentees alike. Nicole, a full professor in a social sciences faculty in an Australian university was mentor to early career researcher Justine. She had been Justine's mentor for two years—a period of time in which Justine had been promoted from Lecturer to Senior Lecturer. Nicole said:

It's really lovely to feel like you are giving something so important to someone else. I see it like a gift, that I received from my own mentor, down the line. This is what it's all about. This is how it should be—taking care of one another. I meet with my mentee once a month. We have lunch and I ask her about how she's going, where she's at with strategies we've worked out for publishing, how her teaching is going, how family life is going. And now, increasingly, the approach to the next promotion. It's the date in my calendar I look forward to the most. She's a lovely person and I like spending that time with her anyway, but it is so satisfying to know that you're doing something of real value, that is worth something to someone else. This is tangible. I learn things from the way she thinks, too.

Bronwen liked to do mentoring in a group setting, so that mentees could not only learn from her, but equally engage in "more parallel mentoring at the same time—some have been with me a while, some I have had only since the start of this year," she explained. From ANU, Bronwen felt that mentoring was best done informally; "I don't need to be taught how to mentor—mentoring I think is just about being generous enough to value other people and let them learn from you. It's an attitude, not a program."

Renata, an associate professor in a US university mathematics department talked about how she approached mentoring with:

what I think is the most important quality of mentoring, and that is being generous with your time and your information with the mentee. Something like this requires not only giving a person what you know—they can get that from anyone, and probably they can get it as a result of their own experience, good and bad, of the institution itself as they move through it. You have to give your time, and think about the person and their particular case, what they need, where they are struggling, and give the benefit of your experience, and that means you must give something of yourself.

Later in the interview, Renata explained to Simone that being generous could be simultaneously rewarding and burdensome:

I'm someone who, as a mentor, is presumed to have the time available to guide someone else through the things that I feel that I had to learn on my own, as a junior member of the university—not this particular one, a different one. I was approached by my own supervisor and asked to be a mentor to a new member of our staff, and also someone who was struggling a little bit. But I don't always *really* have the time—there is always such a lot to do at my stage of career, when you have not yet quite made it but you're not junior or unsuccessful. It's nice when your efforts are recognised, however—and they have been—I mentioned it in my last promotion application. It is also satisfying when you know that what you have done has contributed to someone else's success, and my mentees are very nice about acknowledging that my mentoring has helped them to achieve something.

The generosity of mentors like Renata are key indicators of "good" mentoring—the kind that de Vries (2011) calls "enabling" mentoring, which we described earlier in this work.

Lara, who had been in her Australian university anthropology department for only eighteen months when we interviewed her, explained how she felt this obligation towards her own mentor, for whose time and efforts she was very grateful:

> I don't know how my mentor has time to fit me in, but she always does. She is very senior and seems to be involved in every important executive function of the university—and she does awesome research. She probably doesn't sleep much. I always feel a combination of being thrilled and feeling guilty when I have an appointment with her because I know there's a zillion things she could be doing instead of talking to little old me! She never makes me feel like that on purpose, I should say. But I know how much I owe her. And there are ways I pay it back.

Renata's and Lara's words resonate with Mauss's insights; they problematise the proclaimed goodness of de Vries's "enabling" versions of mentoring in their recognition of the debts they owe their mentors. The fact that these mentees felt the obligation to give back to their mentors raises critical questions about giving that Mauss's work is well-placed, at least initially, to explore.[2] Certainly, it is clear in remarks like Renata's and Lara's that an obligation to return the mentor's gifts is conferred on the mentee. The expectation of return creates a closed circuit of hierarchical relations. Mentors bestow generous gifts on mentees, who are compelled to return the equally given debt. Debts must be paid back in particular ways that sustain the key relations of mentoring. They may, then, be paid back to women in general, or to the mentor herself, or both. As Mauss noted, a gift made of knowledge "enriches both the donor and recipient with the same produce" (1925: 55).

The terms of this "enrichment" were various for our informants. Sometimes, they were literal, as was the case when supervision awards conferred on mentors by an institution required the nomination of the mentee. Such awards were often accompanied by a cash reward, as they are at our own institution; we have both been recipients. Available too is prestige, as such awards are conferred in the context of full ceremonial glory at graduation events. This kind of prestige may be transferrable into hard capital when included in promotion or job applications.

Most often, knowledge reciprocity was expressed as substantive rather than economic gain by mentors when they remarked as Peta did:

I've actually learned quite a lot from my mentee. She's an interesting thinker and she has takes on things that are different from mine. She's very junior to me in terms of where she is in her career, but when I wrote a reference for her last month I made the point that I feel when I engage with her that I am speaking to a much more seasoned colleague than her position and years indicate. I have also told her that some of her insights have made me think differently about my own work. This I think is mentoring at its best; and at its best it is an exchange of knowledge and ideas that benefit both people in the relationship.

The payback might be immediate, as was the case for Geraldine. Geraldine reported that she was "pleased" that she had taken on a mentee "just in time" for the mentee to write a letter to append to her application for promotion to associate professor; the letter had evidenced Geraldine's good institutional citizenship, leadership and practical commitment to gender equity.

Mentees might equally step beyond the temporal parameters of the relationship and "pay forward" their debt, by practically realising and manifesting the investment made in them, mentoring a new generation of junior academic women in their turn. By their success, the mentor's success is confirmed, as genealogies of accomplishment could be built from a founding mentor ancestor; the benefits of a mentor's investment in a mentee could be delivered to the next generation of scholars. Repayments of this variety came with a reciprocal return to the mentor in the form of the satisfaction of elevating all women academics, and the kudos of having done so. This is in fact lauded as one of the principal returns available to senior women and is often expressed as an inducement to participation in mentoring programs.

That practice is certainly not confined to the enclosure of the academy. For example, Michael Stars, a Los Angeles–based apparel company much favored by celebrities recently became a Step Up partner. Step Up is a nonprofit organization that propels girls living in underresourced communities to become "college bound" and "career focused." On Giving Tuesday 2020, as she prepared for the launch of the Step Up campaign, its president, Suzanne Lerner, issued a statement about mentoring that nicely captured its reciprocal qualities in the tropes of generosity and selfishness.

> I was reflecting on how personally rewarding it's been to be a mentor. I've learned that if you mentor someone in an effort to be generous, but don't experience any personal joy from it, then chances are you won't continue to be a mentor. What a loss that would be, not only for those new generations of women and men, but also for you . . . (Lerner, 2020).

The example is one we've deliberately chosen as issuing from an at least ostensibly very different world than the academy; Michael Stars is a fashion house. But the ideal mentees she describes (enthusiastic, curious, hopeful), the reciprocal relations of giving and getting, the translation of invested mentor capital into business success, as well as securing futures for womankind, might just as easily have issued from our own august institution.

GENEROSITY GONE WRONG

Our interviews turned up an abundance of negative mentoring experiences. Stories about how the giving of mentors was not up to scratch or tales of ungrateful or demanding mentees only confirmed for us the importance and centrality of generous giving and grateful receiving. We did collect some "horror stories," as our informant Sue described them, about the shocking abuses that could occur under the guise of mentoring, along with stories about the limits of generosity, as expressed in our next section by another informant, Gemma. Negative stories contained key ideas about the limits of generosity, the delicate balancing point at which giving of one's time began to be taken for granted by the recipient and thus devalued, something defined by the contextual bounds provided by the need to produce teaching and research outputs within a limited time frame. Sue said:

> I know a couple of horror stories about mentoring. This is when it goes really wrong. There was this woman at our place who was mentor to a ridiculous amount of young women. She used to meet them together in her office. Now I know for a fact that not one of those young women got a single useful bit of advice from this woman, because they told me. It was basically her forcing them to sit down for an hour and listening to "my brilliant career." She wouldn't listen to what they might need to know, or what problems they had; it was all about "hey, listen to me!" Such was her ego. Incredible. I was furious when she went for some university position or other that had a gender equity component as part of the role and she had to say what her contributions were—and guess what? She listed all those young women and stole their achievements as though she had had something to do with them. There is nothing about that behaviour that is remotely connected to mentoring, which is meant to be about giving to other people, not taking from them and making it seem like you're the epitome of generosity. I know another one too, from one of my colleagues in the hard sciences, who told me this. She said there was a case—the academic concerned nearly lost her job over it—where an academic started mentoring someone very junior but really, really talented, and basically got her to write up all the papers and do all the grunt work in the labs. And all the while, this was dressed up as mentoring, but that girl got none of the credit. I thought that was appalling.

Tessa, who agreed to talk with us only if she would "never ever" be identified, aimed her sense of transgressed generosity squarely at her mentee. Far more explosively expressive than Sue had been in relating her "horror stories," Tessa exclaimed:

> Mentoring? It's a fucking time suck, is what it is. I have this mentee who is constantly pulling at me for advice and, do you know, the other day she rang me and told me that what she wanted out of our relationship was a job? Absolutely. I can produce that like a magician. Sure. I'll get you a job, missy. She's just post PhD and I get it—it's desperate. You're highly qualified and you don't want a job at a supermarket. But it's just this constant, "can you look at my CV?" "Can you write me a reference?" "Do you know the people at such and such a department?" "Have you got any grants I can be on as your RA?" FUCK OFF. I mean I say it's a time suck because I do actually do that stuff for people, but for her it's like a full-time job *I* should have so *she* can have a full-time job. I should not have agreed to it when she asked me, but I had no idea she'd be so demanding.

Mauss's insights are again useful. In particular, they lay bare how the process of gift exchange in mentoring relationships is underpinned by three obligations: the obligation to give, the obligation to receive and the obligation to reciprocate.

Under the rubric of "power," Dobbins and Fell (2019) argue that a reversal of traditional hierarchical relations between mentor and mentee can occur that is evident only when the scales of generosity presumed in mentoring models falls from hitherto uncritical eyes (see also Clouder & Adefila, 2014: 61). One way in which this might occur is related to the emotional labour and demeanor the mentor must produce in order to appear consistently in the ideal form of the mentor, within the frame of generosity: the wise and nurturing guide. As we have already indicated, such performances might be subject to significant pressure in an already pressurized environment; Polly did not know, exactly, how her mentor Janine kept up such a performance in the context of her already too-busy institutional life. Cracks in the performative façade could seriously impact the encompass of generosity within which mentoring programs are operated. Even Tessa, who found herself utterly infuriated by the demands of her mentee had not expressed her outraged feelings to her mentee. She seethed, swore, resented and raged, but not openly. To do so may have positioned her as unable to give and removed her from the relations of mentoring altogether. That would have denied her the capital on offer, that CV fodder that demonstrates good citizenship and institutional merit, and the basis of her own sense that she did do "those things for women! I support junior women!"

Removal from the role of "giver" could also occur when it was revealed that the mentor's higher claims to expertise were called into question. On such occasions, the mentee could not recognize their better, deeper, longer or more institutionally specific knowledge and expertise as greater or more strategically relevant than their own. This may occur in relationships of mentoring when the mentor is of a different generation, and knows the institution in terms of a past the mentee regards as long gone, or is "stuck in the 1970s," as one mentee complained of her allocated mentor. "God, she's in a total time warp," said Kelly, who had been at an Australian sandstone for six years, of her mentor who was, herself, "regarded as an institution." "She still acts as though she is the undisputed head of a fiefdom," reckoned Kelly, after having received from her mentor some advice about managing a small group of people bound together by area of research interest but, apparently, not by anything else, including the relations of hospitable sociality. "They hate one another," Kelly lamented. "I wanted some advice about people management from someone who had been a department head—what I got was ridiculous." Such mentors had no gifts to bestow.

If mentors had to produce emotional and up-to-date intellectual labour to qualify for an obligation to give, then so too did mentees. Mentees must be, for example, poised as ideal receivers of the wisdom, knowledge and experience that they have indicated by their membership in formal or informal relationships. In Dobbins and Fell's (2019) study of bioscience and nursing mentors and mentee relations, this meant mentees had to be "enthusiastic, confident, assertive and competent," as well as "curious," "inquisitive" and "willing," but not *overly* enthusiastic, annoying, tiresome, irritating, bothersome, or otherwise constitute a nuisance. Especially, they should not be so confident and competent that they revealed themselves inappropriately constituted mentee subjects. An overconfident person might signal that they knew everything already and did not need a mentor (see also Webb & Shakespeare, 2008: 569). Such a signal corrupts the relations of generosity, in that it effectively rejects the proffered gift; to refuse to receive is to reject the social bond.

Clearly, there are conditions for participation in networks of giving and receiving that depend on the giver's capacity to give (and the recognition by mentees of that capacity); the recipient's worthiness to receive gifts, and the capacity of mentees to pay back generosity. But aside from these foundational qualifying characteristics, there were other rules afoot. The fact that there were—and that they were so clearly understood by all parties—raises an important question about generosity in the mentoring context.

CAREFUL REQUESTS FOR GENEROSITY
(OR ASKING THE PRESIDENT FOR
DIRECTIONS TO THE BATHROOM)

In terms of its operations, "enabling" mentoring programs pivot on the notion and the practice of generous giving (Kamvounias, McGrath-Champ & Yip,

2008: 8; Dobbins & Fell, 2019). Mentors need to be "generous" with their time, their advice, their experience, with *themselves*. We collected stories fairly bursting with gratitude for just how much mentors had generously and unselfishly made available to neophyte members of the university, and equally to those who were not new employees but were yet novices in particular roles or offices of the university, or of life: new Heads of School, new supervisors of the HDR or team varieties, those new to balancing motherhood with the demands of a university career. The theme of generosity was consistent, so consistent that it seemed the property of highest value circulating in the practice of mentoring. But generosity did not simply flow unabated between giving mentors and receiving mentees, no matter how well each met the qualifying criteria for participation we have outlined above. There were *rules* for accessing it and for continuing participation in it.

Polly said of her mentor,

> Janine is so giving. I don't know how she has the time. In fact, I know that she doesn't have the time. I feel guilty about taking up so much of her time. I'm so grateful for everything she does for me. I try only to ask her the most important questions I have, and I always, like, thank her profusely. She's so generous and I am really lucky. And guilty!

Polly's friend Rebecca concurred, nodding her agreement with Polly when Simone interviewed the two American Social Science lecturers during a break in the conference they all attended in Norway at the very beginning of 2019.

> It's funny, but as you're talking, Polly, I am remembering that every single email I have written to my mentor starts with "I'm so sorry to disturb you, but I just wondered if I could ask you . . . " I don't think Sally [Rebecca's mentor] has quite the time constraints you're describing Janine has. It's more that she's so important—she does critically important research—and then I appear and want something relatively unimportant, in the stratosphere she inhabits. Don't get me wrong, she has never done anything to make me think I am not important—quite the opposite—but you know what I mean? I feel a bit weird—not quite guilty like you said—but . . . I don't know . . . like a junior senator asking the President where the bathroom is. Or something like that.

Gemma, a sociologist, had a slightly different take. She indicated that the institution itself could step beyond the boundaries of generosity in asking overworked women to become mentors, sometimes. She really liked the idea of mentoring and she'd been approached by her own institution, in Canada, to participate as a successful senior woman. But Gemma was "tired"; she had work "coming out of my ears," and "precious little time" in which to get it all done. Gemma said during her Skype interview,

I think it's really important to support junior women. I know I relied on the support of senior women when I was young; they give you the benefit of their knowledge and their experience. I found for me it was mostly the strategic advice that was important, around publishing and writing grants. However, I really feel at this point of my career [at assistant professor level] that the one thing I truly do not have is time to explain to someone else how to do this. The program requires a very substantial investment of my time straight away, and then in an ongoing way because it's formal and there are workshops and then individual sessions to go to. After that it could probably be more natural and me and the person would work out what suited us, but to be perfectly honest, this formal program approach feels like the university treating my time as free. It already takes so much of it. It feels like theft. What I should do is invoice it!

Lisette, in her early thirties and in a North American history department did not want to be the kind of mentee who was burdensome to her mentor, who was just about to retire; Lisette herself was an early career researcher and had to make sure "that I approach my mentor respectfully as she passes a lifetime of experience over to me." This meant allowing the mentor to set the pace and content of advisements, no matter how much Lisette might want them *now,* to the extent that Lisette did not ask her mentor for advice or meetings. She "gratefully accepted" those opportunities when they presented themselves and did not otherwise bother her mentor.

As the foregoing excerpts reveal, positioning oneself to receive the generosity of mentors had to be done with a great deal of care—the kind of care one would take if one had to enquire of the president the location of the nearest bathroom. Mentees trod carefully, respectfully, even with trepidation.

The generosity that defines the intention and the ideal practice of mentoring must, apparently, be carefully, *carefully* made manifest. Mentees shouldn't take too much of a mentor's time or capacities, lest the mentee feel guilty, or the mentor become agitated by demands that are too great. Mentors shouldn't be asked by their institutions to give too much to mentoring, lest it feels like taking—like theft. Mentors should not take too much from their mentees, lest they begin to practice intellectual theft, or accord to themselves the fruits of the labour they did not undertake, falsely representing generosity. Demands made by mentees on time and resources, demands made by mentors of their mentees, and demands made by universities of mentors had to be put in cautious terms. The university could not compel a senior female academic to become a mentor, but it could articulate the benefits for mentees, for the university, for women in general and for the mentor herself in terms of generosity, and make an appeal to a mentor to "make a difference to someone's career and life," or "make the university a better place for women to work," or "take up the opportunity to pass your wisdom and experience on," or to 'be involved in making a new generation of strong, successful women."

The delicacy required in approaching a mentor was clear in what mentees told us. Advisements abounded: "don't take up more of their time than they have offered, leave a meeting or phone call at the agreed time." "Never make them schedule the meeting. You do that." "Don't do star fucking [appear awe-struck and fawning]. Be grateful and respectful. There's a difference." "Always thank them for the time you took up out of their day." "Don't ask them every little thing you ever wanted to know. It's a long-term thing—pace yourself, and them." These advisements and cautions, we found, are formalized by professional mentoring companies, such as PeopleGrove, an organization that "helps institutions bring personalized, mentor-focused communities to students and alumni from enrollment to long after graduation" (2020). Featured on the page in June 2020 was "Robert," who wanted a job after graduating university. He told PeopleGrove that the key to being a successful mentee was

> generosity, the giving mindset, that's important. But it's sort of a paradox that you also have to be totally open to receiving as well. So if you come in either just expecting to get stuff for nothing, or if you come in thinking "I'm not worthy, I'm here to worship at the altar of this more experienced person." Neither of those approaches works. You need to be giving and receiving with equal zeal.

Robert equally advised that care must be taken in making demands of mentors, and the company made graphics of the recommendations to accompany the story that resonated with what we heard from our own mentee informants.

Mentors are also subject to rules or norms, as their best practice advisements to us clearly indicate: "don't exploit a mentee," "don't overwhelm someone with everything you know all at once," "think about what they need to know that is most useful for them, rather than telling them what you think is the most useful advice," "try to not use 'I' all the time—as in 'I' did this, I did that, I think this is the most important thing you can do," ask instead, "what kinds of things do YOU want to achieve? Who do you want to be?," "if you don't think the match is right, be honest about it," "If you don't have enough time to be an effective mentor for someone, don't participate—it will only make the person feel like they are not worth it at a time when they are signaling that they need support," "be generous with your time," "A mentee is not your slave," and so on.

At the Australian National University, mentors have to apply to be mentors, to ensure that they are equipped and able to offer a useful, well-matched experience for the mentee. This was the case for most formal mentoring programs instituted by universities across the West that follow an "invitation only" model. Alison is a successful applicant and is listed as a formal mentor on ANU's website. Duly vetted, she is qualified to mentor her charges about:

Balancing research with high teaching load;
HDR candidate supervision;
Teaching strategies;
Getting promoted;
ARC DECRA and/or Future Fellowship;
Non-government funding;
Leading teams;
Navigating university politics;
Managing difficult professional relationships and
Outreach and community engagement.

Should prospective mentees want to be mentored by Alison, they would not simply be able to approach her; they would have to submit a form expressing their preference for Alison, and two other potential mentors, another formal rule governing the program. The presence of a set of understandings or rules around the approaches mentors and mentees might make to one another that was not peculiar to any particular institution, and even appeared on mentoring websites in handy chart form, raised a question for us: *If generosity is so fundamental to mentoring, and if mentors were distinguished by their capacity and willingness to give to mentees, then why do people have to be so careful about asking for it? Why, indeed, does it have to be requested at all?*

Australian anthropologist Nicolas Peterson encountered a similar curiosity when, in the mid-1990s he reexamined fieldnotes he had taken among Yolngu (Murngin) Aboriginal people in the 1960s. In his published reflections on his notes, Peterson (1993) disputes the idea that hunter-gatherer societies operate principally in accordance with an ethic of generosity that takes the form of unsolicited giving. This is in sharp contrast to the views advanced by Sahlins (1972) and Hiatt (1982) who had declared generosity "the highest secular value" operating in Aboriginal Australia (1982: 14–15). If that were so, Peterson wondered, why did he document so many demands being verbally and nonverbally put? If generosity was so highly valued, why did people have to constantly demand it? The fact that he bore witness not to unsolicited giving but in fact a kind of taking that involved "testing behaviour," "assertive behavior" and/or substantiating behavior meant that Peterson had to regard generosity as pure, one way giving a Western [ethnographer's] presumption.[3]

We too reconsider generosity on analysis of the form and content of requests to be mentored—the rules for inclusion—not only in institutional context but in the much broader context of the business world generally. We do not think that generosity is absent; rather, as we have suggested in the foregoing, generosity is not straightforwardly generous. It entails mentors and mentees firmly in hierarchical relations of power, in which mentors occupy positions enabling giving, and mentees receive and repay those gifts.

The presence of expectations of willing and equipped, appropriately constituted receivers and gift givers, and the expectation of the reciprocation of gifts makes sense of the presence of rules pertaining to entering the relations of generosity. We might liken this to the nonmaterial gift of hospitality, an ancient and contemporary virtue in which one cares for the needs of the stranger, what Finley (1982) calls the general human obligation to hospitality.[4] While the original meaning of hospitality is based on reciprocity and mutual exchange—just as strangers may need you, you might need them at some future time, and therefore you should offer them hospitality—the seeker of hospitality must take great care in requesting it (see Pitt-Rivers, 1968). That is, in order for a gift to be a righteous act it must presume an ability on the part of the recipient to participate in such a relationship. That ability is described by Bourdieu as the "recognition of the partner to whom, in the particular case, it [a gift] accords equality in honour" (1990: 100). Only parties equipped to reciprocate might gain admittance to the relationship. Demand sharing is a complex behavior that is not predicated simply on need.

The careful approaches one must make—institutionally, as mentee and mentor—to gaining entry into the exchange of gifts are instructive, indicating the lively negotiations implied and practiced within it. It permits, as Peterson once said of the Yolgnu, the opportunity to test out the state of a relationship between two parties and whether or not they are fit to give and receive the valuable gifts of mentoring. They equally provide the initial basis for the establishment of such a relationship, as is clearly indicated in the fact that mentors and mentees must either be screened institutionally, or, as indicated in the PeopleGrove advisements, engage in a "flash" meeting to establish a match. The relations of mentoring cannot be presumed to simply stretch forward unproblematically over time. The must instead be produced and reproduced and maintained by social action that is undertaken in accordance with the expectations of generous exchanges. Undergirding exchanges is the founding and the production of a community.

Maintaining generous exchanges secures and reproduces a community that, for Colley (2003) produces the conditions for class consciousness. In her book-length treatment of mentoring in hierarchical contexts, *Mentoring for Social Inclusion: A Critical Approach to Nurturing Mentor Relationships* the overriding message is that female experience of institutions can never be disentangled from the wider power relations that envelop and entail those involved in its operations. Colley's work traces the history of mentoring and examines mentoring in practice through the narratives proffered by participants in mentoring programs themselves. Revealed in and through them are the complex power dynamics of the mentor relationship, including the place of mentoring against the background policy-driven schemes and social inequalities, the emotional cost of mentoring, and the counterproductive outcomes it can produce. In Colley's offering, narratives are given a leading role—not only in terms of the window they offer into experience, but also as a mobilising force that will, if correctly deployed, change things for women institutional participants.

Colley's work undertakes an interrogation of narratives collected in situ, an investigation that reveals consistently emergent themes of grievance. For Colley, the consistency of grievances offers up the possibility for narratives to turn from descriptions of painful experiences into therapeutic talk in collectivity and thereafter into action: that is, a consciousness of sharing common grievances against the patriarchy has the capacity to unite senior and junior women in a collective struggle fought with the corrective weapon of mentoring. This classic Marxian analysis puts the view that women become conscious of sharing common grievances against the beneficiaries of patriarchal organisation, thus forming a class, of sorts, "in itself." So mentoring provides an arena for sharing and shaping these grievances and becomes a means for addressing them.

For Dobbins and Fell (2019) mentoring produces robust knowledge transfers across generations, creating a genealogical community. And, Devos (2008) warns that they can produce a continuation of the patriarchal community in its reproduction of the values of "masculine" institutions.

Reproductions of the communities that mentoring builds in whatever way they are envisaged are subject to fracture. Should the gifts of the mentor become redundant or less worthy, should the capacity of the mentee to reciprocate the gifts diminish, or should the mentee's worthiness as a recipient deteriorate, the relationship might also disappear on the basis that it is unable to produce the relations of generosity. But most of all, as Peterson also notes of his Yolngu material, the giving of gifts to others who in both cases of mentoring and demand sharing, *creates communities characterized by status asymmetry.*

LOUDLY PROCLAIMED GIFTS

Analyzing mentor relationships by recourse to Mauss's work permits us a reassessment of the position of the one-way transfer of generous gifts from mentors to mentees. From a Derridean perspective, the gift of mentoring ceases to become a gift at all; a gift is only a gift if it does not obligate and incur debt. The gift that comes with obligation and debt becomes, instead, commodity, and it is only ever possible to gift when a gift is not recognized as such. Derrida (1992) has argued that Mauss's thesis actually remains firmly within the logic of contract and exchange; the gift practically functions as a commodity. Once recognized, the gift bestows a debt on the recipient that can be annulled only through an appropriate, suitable form of return (12–14). It is precisely this economy of contract and exchange between self-present individuals that makes generosity impossible. Only in invisible silence does generosity do its work of personal and social formation.

The loud proclamations of the generous giving of mentors, the value of their gifts to mentees, and the acknowledgement of the debt mentees owe their mentors stand in stark contrast to the idea that true giving takes place only in invisibility or silence. It furthers our thesis that a logic of exchange and contract, hierarchically arrayed, characterizes "enabling" forms of mentoring.

FORGOTTEN CONTRIBUTIONS

Derrida's insights into the forgetting of generosities also contribute to our thesis of exchange. The memorialization of mentors' gifts is made in perpetuity—appearing in promotion applications, on curricula vitae, in institutional rewards. As senior women mentors' contributions are memorialized, mentees contributions are forgotten; their repayments are pressed into the service of memorializing the mentor. In such terms, mentors might be said to replicate patriarchal operations, in which women make their contributions in the terms of value set by men. Such are the conditions of what Roslyn Diprose calls "virtuous giving" (2002).

Diprose emphasizes how "virtuous giving" memorialises only those who are in possession of something worthy enough to give, and how it equally erases or forgets those who are in positions only to receive. Forgotten recipients include the marginalised—they might be the landless, the unemployed, the indigenous, the immigrant—who depend for their inclusion in dominant systems on the generous giving of donors. Donors equip the marginalised with the skills, experiences, access and knowledge to participate in these dominant systems, as is the case in enabling mentoring, where career development and networks are made available to inexperienced mentees by their successful mentors.

Diprose argues that the receivers of generous gifts are forgotten in very particular terms. Virtuous giving is done unidirectionally, from donor to donee, in the service of drawing the donee into the world of the donor. Donees are donees precisely because they lack something that the donor is in a position to give. As that (experience, knowledge, *nous*, insight) is given by the donor, the difference between the donee and the donor reduces. At no time does the donor have to value the difference of the donee from herself; it is the difference of the donee that is the trouble in the first place. It is what must be reduced in order for the donee to succeed. In the context of mentoring, we might say that our task as mentors is to produce successful women, women who are just like us, as successful as us, *the same as us*. It is the alterity of the donee, the mentee, that for Diprose is forgotten: virtuous giving values "my" experience over yours because your difference is rendered deficient—it is the thing that must be reduced so that you can be successful. Thus, the difference of the donee is valueless.

Diprose's insights have obvious implications for white treatment of indigenous people (indeed one of the case studies she rehearses concerns white relations with Indigenous Australians), but the same kind of assimilationist problem applies equally to mentoring relationships that are made and sustained through the relations of virtuous giving. Notably, the rendering of mentees "the same" as the successful mentor has significant implications for the claim of the achievement of gender equity goals. Mentor women are successful in the patriarchal terms set out for success; making mentee women over into patriarchally endorsed selves reduces the possibilities for critically engaging those terms and leaves only replication available.

To counter the hierarchising effects of virtuous generosity, Diprose proposes the alternative operation of corporeal generosity, in which the alterity of the other is valued. It has the capacity and opportunity to challenge the successful self and the conditions under which that self was made successful. Such challenges provide opportunity for hierarchical relations—here mentoring relations—to take more equitable forms. Such rearrangements might produce institutional gender equity in a way that virtuous giving cannot; indeed, virtuous generosity, with its emphasis on the emulation of successful mentors who have mastered the male standard of success invariably maintains and cements patriarchal hierarchies.

DIFFERENCE

In mentoring programs, generosity appears as a virtue that leads a mentor to give what they have to mentees within an exchange economy. Within them, generosity is understood as an individual virtue that, en masse, creates the net effect of benefit for women in the institution. But it masks how the making junior women over into our own images as successful senior women undergirds patriarchal continuity.

In Diprose's (2002) formulation, the virtuous generosity upon which mentoring programs depend can never produce a system change, like levelling the institutional playing field for women, as is a desired result of mentoring programs.[5] This is because virtuous generosity must be repaid; it belongs to and enlivens an economy of exchange in which the generous gifts that mentors give must be repaid by mentees. Given and consumed in mentoring programs are ideas and practices that will assist women to achieve success in the institution that is tilted against female accomplishment. In spite of the odds, mentors have achieved that success. According to the ANU website, which lists handpicked mentors, they can, for example, teach mentees how to achieve publication success, attain promotion, get grants, and balance work with childcare—all of which tend to be more difficult for women than men. The basis of the mentoring relationship is that the knowledge so generously given is unidirectional: the mentee does not get to change the outlook of the mentor, as the mentor aims to do to the mentee. This means that there is no chance of producing anything but success in the form it presently comes in: male.

Diprose proposes a different kind of generosity, one based in alterity. In Diprose's formulation, generosity is, in its essence, becoming open to the other. Openness is one's own awareness that the other is different from the self, and the awareness that, to the other, the self is different. That is, the self appears as an other to the other. In this openness, the subjectivities that encounter each other share their alterity as gifts. In that exchange, people re-form their identities in relation to others, or, in Diprose's terms, "disperse their identities into their others." In a generous exchange with the other,

> the alterity that animates perception . . . opens my movement toward the other without promise of returning the same and allows the other into the singularity of subjectivity that it has inspired (185).

Thus, my subjectivity is opened to the possibility of transformation and the other is allowed subjectivity and a possibility of similar transformations of that subjectivity.

The notion that self is dispersed into the other has a great deal in common with Derrida's conceptualisation of différance (1978 [1967]), especially in the sense that différance constitutes identity *and* difference, in the same kinds of terms that Diprose applies to generosity:

> Self-identity, a manner of being, cannot be constituted without a production of an interval or a difference between the self and the other. No self-present identity, no relation to Being, is generated without this relation to the other. . . . As one's identity and social value are produced through a differentiation between the self and the other then the identity of the self is dispersed into the other (7).

This kind of openness is closed down when it is encompassed inside the parameters of exchange economies, within which gifts are exchanged. This is because such economies are governed by an expectation that what has been given to the other must be returned *unchanged* by that other's difference from the self. This enclosure occurs, too, as a direct result of the circulation of gifts.

Derrida defines the gift as "the impossible" because it is always made and enclosed within the parameters of the exchange economy. Gifts circulate with the expectation that they retain their base value, and it is on this basis that a debt is given in the gift when it is made by donor to donee, as it is in mentoring practice. It is never, then, truly given away, for value must return to the giver—the institution, then the mentor in our case. It is thus annulled by the structure in which it is enclosed—and that is the aporia of the gift (Derrida, 1992: 6–27).

The results of this conceptualisation are applicable to mentoring. As Mauss noted, a gift made of knowledge "enriches both the donor and recipient with the *same* produce" (1925: 55, our emphasis). What is exchanged in mentoring programs, between mentor and mentee? Between program and institution? We have argued throughout that what is exchanged is knowledge—the knowledge of how to be, how to walk and talk, how to understand, manage and reproduce the (male) standards expected, how to exempt oneself from them, how to do the calculations that support exemption, how to maintain the proper emotional demeanour in and through which proper academic performances are turned in, how to teach, how not to do things, and, most importantly of all, how to participate in the knowledge economy in the patriarchal terms in which that participation is constituted and valued. Within the terms of these exchanges, what is returned is not altered by a potentially transformative encounter with an other. Instead, mentees are the recipients of generous gifts—of knowledge regarding the navigation of the patriarchal institution. They accrue this knowledge and at a certain point—when they have demonstrated their success in navigating the system—*nous* becomes intuition, second nature, accrued wisdom. That accrual can be passed on to novices in the form of advisements and strategies with which they can conduct their own navigations, thus replicating and undergirding the position of women as recipients of male assistance. It is here that generosity, when considered in the terms of exchange economies, seeks to enclose difference as lesser. An enduring exchange relation becomes paradigmatic and reproduces itself as community.

Injustice results when the operations of generosity are governed by the way social norms and values (in this case pertaining to gender, success and seniority) determine which bodies are recognized as possessing property that can be given and which bodies are devoid of property and so can only benefit from the generosity of others, and which bodies are worthy of gifts and which are not—as we have indicated, this signalling is complex in the university context, where processes and practices underscored by neutrality and merit-based assessments are yet attended by gendered presumptions.

This returns us to our original thesis, that the generosity involved in mentoring serves to place women within an enclosure of institutional replication that flattens, rather than produces, the differences between male and female members of the institution. With it are flattened the potentials for changing the patriarchal operations of the institution, even as they pop up as possibilities in the changing physical environs of the university, the statistics that indicate rises in the employment participation of women, even as it permits women to wield "the patriarchy" as a weapon against sexist men they encounter within its bounds, even as it pops up in recognitions of female bodies as different and exemptible in the form of corporeal accounting.

This, equally, returns us to our thesis regarding the original Mentor; namely that his principal role was to *reduce* the potential difference between the patriarchal regime overseen by Odysseus and the one that would be inherited by Telemachus in the event that Odysseus failed to return from the Trojan War. It is in and through this revelatory understanding of the importance of difference—but difference that is enfolded into the self—that it becomes obvious that mentoring, although it seems on first pass based on operations of generosity—might in fact be part of the problem.

Alterity is important in Diprose's workings because generosity constructs identity in and through the corporeal immediacy of experiencing the other; it is "subjectivity as sensibility animated by the other's alterity" (187). Sensibility—the corporeal experience of others and the world more broadly—is motivated by the other's difference. Subjectivity and identity re-forming themselves in relation to alterity—and that can go either way; it might produce a generous transformation of social imaginaries, or a very parsimonious reinforcement of them, in which the other's subjectivity is enclosed, and closed off.[6]

Could it be different?

NOTES

1. We invoke this term on purpose, to set the reader in mind of the enclosure in which women are contained, even when generosity veneers debt relations. Hierarchical relations persist, just as this phrase does, bringing with it all the connotations of women's station.

2. We know as we write our book that we are asking readers to do some difficult things, not the least of which is to suspend the idea that mentoring is straightforwardly an act of good citizenship. As will become clear, we are also asking something outrageous: we're asking for a suspension of the idea that generosity might be, at its core, "good." We think that the difficulty associated with suspending these assumptions may be why mentoring has not been subject to deep and sustained critique.

3. In particular, Peterson notes that because the unsolicited giving associated with generosity by Westerners is seen as positive, the practice of demand sharing is seen as

negative, since it is a damper on that generosity. But should the practice be construed negatively? Peterson thinks not.

4. We cannot resist noting that in Homer's *Odyssey* the rule of hospitality was to welcome a guest into the home, offer him food and shelter, and only afterwards ask questions about his person and mission.

5. This is, fundamentally, an openness to others—a necessary (pre)condition to sociality and social formation. It is not, she contends, a character trait that might be leveraged to greater or lesser effect in individual or collective (i.e., institutional, social) contexts; she situates giving ontologically, politically and sociologically. Her position is one that attempts to promote ways to foster social relations that recognise difference and its relationship to identity, community and generosity. Diprose's position springs at first from well-established philosophically informed conceptualisations of intercorporeality, particularly those rehearsed by Nietzsche, Merleau-Ponty and Levinas—as indicated in the work's title. The self is, in such conceptualisations, always and already "given" to others and founds a generosity that predates a socio-political ethical practice. Within critical phenomenology, generosity takes on an ontological sense as openness toward, or being-given to, others characteristic of human subjectivity, interrelationality, and justice within social and political relations. The "corporeal" component of corporeal generosity highlights both the affective basis of the generosity by which human beings are interrelated and the significance of bodily markers of differences between human beings. The ethical dimension of corporeal generosity lies in its sense as potentiality toward equitable and just social relations; conversely, forgetting.

6. This evokes Gatens's (1996) concept of social imaginaries upon which Diprose draws to develop her own conceptualisations of identity and community formation. At the heart of Gaten's "social imaginary" is the examination of the processes that inform and reform the categorisation of individual and collective bodies, and in particular the terms in which they are valued (and devalued). The predeterminations and judgements to which bodies are subject are evident in their departure from heteronormative masculinity. These take the forms of devalued female gender identity, any nonheterosexual orientation, and any deviation away from "health." These and other categorisations that acquire devalued status stand as social imaginaries that "already memorialize the generosity of the privileged and forget and do not actively perceive the giving of others" (192). That is, as a function of their devalued status, people in those categories stand relative to those in a central, normative one as recipients of generous donation: as donees. If people are included in participations, it is resultant of a decision to permit participation, to allow inclusion. Such relations undergird social imaginaries as they stand and constitute and make manifest a parsimonious relation to the world and others. For social imaginaries imagined precisely in the terms of donor-donee relations to be deconstructed and rebuilt in other terms, a different version of generosity is required. Openness is the key to transformation, itself enabled by the transformation of cultural conventions that do not presently admit "different modes of being" in terms any other than their relative hierarchical, current, positions as donees (Gatens, 193). The facile charm of "inclusion" cannot masquerade as openness, for it would remain a decision of the virtuous to generously include the other. It

is only when openness becomes possible that social imaginaries interested in devaluation lose their organising power and their own value, that the operations of social justice, equality and inclusion find their true and enduring forms. This occurs when objective measures demonstrate that such qualities are equally available to people regardless of their different modes and styles of being, be they sexual, gendered or cultural.

Conclusion

COULD IT BE DIFFERENT?

For want of a better word, "technically," it could be different. That is, theoretically, a sound basis exists for doing generosity in different terms—and, actually, for turning the world upside down, righting wrongs, dealing with injustices. If existing social, institutional norms affect the recognition of generosity: "parsimony and social injustice rest on memorializing the generosity of some while forgetting the giving of others" (75). Thus, it is important to focus on the mutuality of exchanges—and that means, following Derrida, that a gift is only possible if it is not recognised as such and thus escapes being commodified and creating a sense of debt to the giver (Derrida, 1992: 6–27; Diprose, 2002: 6). For Diprose, attempting to figure generosity in terms of the exchange economy, where debt and expectancy of return create a closed circuit, fails, because the self is never truly opened to the other and what is given of the self is expected to be returned as if untouched (184). As we have noted, mentoring is considered to be a generous act—an instinctual categorisation because it entails a choice to work with those less equipped, less experienced. This, however, remains within the enclosure of virtuous generosity which, as Diprose notes, invokes and materialises "a habit of giving some of what I already have to others in my own terms, a habit of expressing at the same time as confirming my own socially bound way of being as if it were finished" (192). Somehow, the rigid confines of the social imaginary of being closed to the other, and some others in particular, must be broken open.

For Diprose, the break comes when generosity is abandoned as a virtue that constitutes giving as a wilful process from the more equipped and resourced persons to those less able, and occurs instead as a process in which both participants are afforded property that can be and is mutually given and received. Significantly, insofar as mentoring is concerned, generosity is fundamentally considered transformational—but not as a result of helping those one wishes to make over so that they become more "like me." It is instead transformational because the other can effectively contribute to the construction of the self. Generosity, for Diprose, is based in the formation and construction of community and it "bases community formation on the production and transformation of differences rather than on assumptions of commonness" (2002: 13).

Diprose has already rehearsed how a generous transformation of communities might work, in Australia. Indeed, the circumstances afoot in Australia impelled her call for the generous transformation of communities. She points out that Australia's deeply—and deeply "ordinary"—nationalist political climate bases community formation on presumptions of common ethnicity, to the extent that we can speak, and in quite distinct terms, "Aboriginal community," "immigrant community," "white community," and subsets thereof, of each. These stand in sharp dissimilarity, evident otherness, from one another and, as they do, they reproduce the social imaginaries that had (? Have?) their bases in biological difference. What is needed for transformation is trouble: specifically, only if communities are troubled by some difference can they "admit other ways of seeing and being . . . only if alterity always troubles the social imaginaries from within their expression, through intercorporeal perception, acts, and gestures, could it be said that these imaginaries and the bodies that gain privilege from them are open to transformation and to different ways of being" (Diprose, 2002: 186). New relations between these groups would depend on two things: first, the opening of a willingness to the other's difference to craft the (unfinished) self, and second, the removal of the structures of generous exchange that would see "welfare," "donorship" or "permission" to participate in the arena of white privilege for the basis for encounters of the 'different' other. Hence, new relations rely upon that which the other gives in the thick of her very difference. This is another way of saying that generosity is not governed by economic logic. It must therefore produce excess beyond this logic; the excess that opens the self for others is what is left outside of that logic: the *in*calculable, the *un*accounted for: and this is another way of saying that one must be prepared to accept that the other's difference, and that which she has to offer, might fall outside expectations, and will not need to conform to the form of a repayment of donor generosity (50–51).

In mentoring context, this means that "commonness," that is, the presumption that permission to participate in the patriarchy, and generous donations of assistance to accomplish that, must be abandoned in favour of "community." The identity of its members cannot be limited to participation within a matrix of any social imaginary that would define relations between generous donors and indebted donees—whether they be institution and women, or mentors and mentees.

So: we could do it. But we could do lots of other things, too, that would even up gender inequities, or in some way or another make for a better world. David Graeber has thought before about how we could do things that would radically improve the lives of others—he has considered the apparent possibility of doing something like changing capitalism, and in particular changing how we might think about and operationalise the notion of debt. Changing it, says Graeber, is exceptionally difficult—even though we know about the dire effects it can have on people's lives. Graeber thinks so because of the moral stance people take on debt and particularly the ferocity of opinion surrounding the obligation to pay back what one owes. In his 2013 interview with *Boston Review* reporter David Johnson, Graeber speaks of "the strange moral power that debt has over people," demonstrated especially well after the 2008 global economic crash:

> David Graeber: [There is a moral presumption that] all debts ought to be repaid. Actually, no, debts don't really need to be repaid . . . debts can be made to disappear. Once you understand that the narrative we've been handed has been false, you'd think this would be the moment when you start thinking about larger questions: Why do we have an economy? What is debt? What is money? How could these things be organized differently? . . . So I think one of the questions I'm asking . . . is not just about the power of debt but also why we come to see debt—exchange whereby complete transactions are debts—as being the essence of all social relations, because the very logic of exchange is just one of many ways that we ourselves think of the morality of distribution and transfer of material goods . . . the moment you realize that everything we're doing is not an exchange, suddenly you realize that forms of feudal hierarchy actually exist right here, but forms of communism also exist right here. Almost any social possibility already exists and is part of the daily fabric of our existence. We're just taught not to notice it or think it's particularly important.

Note that Graeber makes two key points in his interview with Johnson. First, he notes that the realisation that economic narratives are false can lead to a critical questioning of the moral obligation to repay debt. Second, that critical questioning often *does not* lead to a sustained critique that produces change. There is a broader point in the offing here, namely that the systems, things and organising principles acquire a power drawn from and maintained by their disassociation with us—to the extent that they acquire their own lives and come to govern us. As Miller (2005) has observed, a society may gradually develop all manner of systems, over time: economic systems, governance systems, education systems. Incorporation in those systems furnishes members with the knowledge to reproduce them (schooling of course is a primary example), and these understandings accumulate over generations. Persons are created through these processes (again, one can see that education systems are a prime example, involvement in which concerns the whole person, not just the "portion" that became educated). Each of these forms "will tend to its own self-aggrandisement and interests. Education may become institutionalised as a system increasingly geared to its own interests. It may become an oppressive single sex boarding school whose sadistic staff cripple rather than build the capacity of its pupils" (Miller, 2005: 8). It might, equally, take the form of an economic system that seems to be so powerful it produces its own specific requirements that must be tended. To not do so would mean disaster, as real lives fail to prosper, or even survive. But as Graeber says, that system has become so powerful that questioning its veracity becomes unthinkable, and changing it becomes nigh on impossible—even when it might mean making lives more tenable, more viable. Even tending to its component parts in ways alternative to that which is usually done becomes too difficult to even contemplate.

This does not bode well for the prospect of considering, then changing, the production of the institution. We might be able to see the problems, we might not say, "this system is the best." In common with defenders of capitalism, who do not say, "Yes, . . . [capitalism is] actually better." They realize that they can't. They're just saying, *"All right, it's not the best system in the world, but no other system is possible anyway"*(see Johnson, 2013, our emphasis). Or is it?

The effect of COVID-19 on institutional patriarchy has been profound: women's disadvantage has been very significantly accelerated as a result of the pandemic. Medical ethicist Keymanthri Moodley and political scientist Amanda Gouws for example note that:

> The COVID-19 pandemic and the consequent public health response of lockdown has brought into sharp relief the constraints faced by women across the board. We have been keeping a keen eye on the impact it's having on women in academia—our field of work and research. What we're observing, and what's being backed up by research, is that women are facing additional constraints as a result of COVID-19. These range from the added burdens and responsibilities of working from home, through to the fact that fewer women scientists are being quoted as experts on COVID-19, all the way to far fewer women being part of the cohort producing new knowledge on the pandemic. None of these constraints are new. Earlier research confirms that women academics carry large teaching burdens, with relatively little time for research and publication compared to their male colleagues, many of whom do not carry equivalent domestic responsibilities. Increased pressure on women academics caused by the COVID-19 pandemic is magnifying this fractured landscape of gender parity in academia. The impact is being felt in terms of productivity. This is manifesting itself in terms of public exposure, knowledge generation and who is being called on to provide advice (Moodley & Gouws, 2020).

Pieces like this are now very common. There appears to be generalised agreement that women academics (and indeed women generally) have suffered under pandemic conditions in ways that men have not. Many, too, have suggested that the sharpness of the disadvantage could provoke a new institutional gender order. As Canadian economist Armine Yalnizyan suggests of new orders more broadly, economic recovery without a deep "she-covery" would be inadequate; such a recovery would mean supporting women to return to work not only by providing things like state-supported child care, but ditching the presumption that women should be primary caregivers to children in the first instance (see Gaviola, 2020). Within and beyond the academy, one strand of conversation has been along the lines that men have unavoidably come to understand what it might be like to have their careers disrupted by the needs of their children, as a result of the initial need for people to remain in lockdown. However, this understanding might not have been conferred in any substantive manner, since, as a result of the operations of the patriarchy, decisions about furloughing and taking redundancy packages have been taken on the basis of which partner earns less. For heterosexual couples, that's been the female partner. For couples with kids, deciding to stay home has very often been necessary, as childcare has become unaffordable, or is not being offered. The Institute for Fiscal Studies (IFS) and University College London (UCL) interviewed 3,500 families and found that women were doing far more of the childcare than were men when both partners were working from home and had roughly the same work requirements and expectations, or when both parents were out of work. Paula Sheridan, a business coach who was interviewed by the BBC for its 29 May newscast remarked that this was hardly surprising, because "the [male] partner has no idea that all of this stuff even happens, because he has needed to."

Nevertheless, as IFS Deputy Research Director Sonya Krutikova notes of data emerging from the Institute of Fiscal Studies/UCL project:

> Fathers, on average, are doing nearly double the hours of childcare they were doing prior to the crisis. This may bring about changes in the attitudes of fathers, mothers, children and employers about the role of fathers in meeting family needs for childcare and domestic work during the working week (quoted in Webber, 2020).

Perhaps such indications as these underscore Diprose's thesis, that corporeal generosity is the result of an openness to alterity. Perhaps it is the case that violent conditions visited upon us by the pandemic have forced hitherto unknown appreciations for the lived experiences of those who are "other" to "us"—to the extent that their experiences might be able to change "our" lives. Or, perhaps the effects of COVID-19 that have seen women suffer disproportionate job and income losses (largely because of their overrepresentation in the hardest-hit sectors of the economy, and because it's often cheaper for women to give up work to cover the cost of childcare when men on average earn more) will reinforce the way things are now.

There are some grounds for hope—if not a sustained hope, then one that is realised at least for a moment. At the very beginning of our book, we suggested that the unwelcome arrival of the COVID-19 pandemic has made plain how neoliberalism has failed some institutional members. We gave the example of the casual labour force, whose predicament was fully appreciated only in the precise moment of its demise. It was appreciated precisely because full-time academics suddenly had to contemplate what it would be like to have to assess coursework assignments within the short timeframe normally given to casual employees. It felt unbearable. Suddenly, the casual staff members' situation could be felt; suddenly, their predicament could be fully realised. Could the same possibility arise between academic men and women?

We suggested earlier, by recourse to David Graeber's 2013 remarks about changing ideas about indebtedness, that things look a bit grim on the structural change front. However, this apparently infertile ground might be just the place to look. In his book *I Am Dynamite* (2003), Nigel Rapport explores how power is conventionally regarded as being held by social institutions. These, evidently, determine the conditions of our lives, set up our life chances, and predict a great deal about who we will be. But to find power, Rapport instead looks into the circumstances of some ostensibly disempowered lives—including the life of the writer and Auschwitz survivor Primo Levi, and the refugee and engineer Ben Glaser. He explores the ways in which, as disempowered as they might initially appear, each of the lives he examines avoid the big power structures to effectively power their own life projects. We too want to look for evidence that things might change for women in the unlikeliest of places—feeling, as Rapport does, that so doing makes for a much more compelling case. We went, vicariously through Lina AbiRafeh, Executive Director of the Arab Institute for Women (AiW) at the Lebanese American University, to contexts that she says are far more patriarchally inclined. AbiRafeh notes:

> The Arab region holds very traditional, largely patriarchal, views of what constitutes "productivity." Labor, both domestic and professional, is gendered, with women relegated to traditionally "feminine" roles. This feminization of women's work places both women and men at a disadvantage, creating an artificial juxtaposition between what is valued and what is not. With everyone now working from home, domestic divisions of labor are brought into plain view. In the Arab region, there is also less shared housework and parenting. We could use this time at home for men to take on an equal share of household work and childcare—"jobs" previously relegated to women. The global "sudden spike in

childcare" is currently being felt by women, but men now have the opportunity to step up and play a greater role in the lives of their children. Will it happen in the Arab region? I'm not so sure. But the opportunity is there (AbiRafeh, 2020: np).

Our offering has explored multiple manifestations of mentoring, including the named, formal, programmatic version that was the subject of our last chapter. Across this work, we have taken the view that mentoring occurs in more situations than named versions of the practice. Indeed, we have based our work around the idea that mentoring could be said to occur when women are given advisements about their institutional positionedness, and clues about how to navigate it. We have also demonstrated that in all its forms, mentoring tends to undergird patriarchal conditions. Using these notions, we have been able to examine the ways in which, for example, institutional buildings exert patriarchal influence over women members. We have found the presence of Athena in built forms, and even taking up her own named form as Athena SWAN. In all of its manifestations, mentoring has been in the business of reproducing patriarchal forms and making institutional bodies over into persistent foundational male models. Our analysis demonstrates how mentoring (ironically) undergirds and replicates the patriarchal structures it seeks to trouble. Across the preceding substantive chapters, we have worriedly produced our argument, that mentoring is in the business of replication, reproduction, imitation, mimicry. What would it take to trouble the production of sameness, that includes the making over of women into the institutionally preferred forms that "we" already take, and thus the reproduction of the institution as we presently know it?

Perhaps it will take a pandemic. Perhaps that pandemic will be insufficient as a catalyst. What is clear is that the university will not be able to carry on in the form with which we are familiar. If nothing else, the pandemic has demonstrated the limits of the political and economic conditions that have, since the 1980s reforms, sustained the sector (see Jayasuriya, 2020, for a comprehensive analysis of these conditions as they relate to university governance and future economic prospects of the sector). Things will have to change—and perhaps it will no longer be in the best institutional interests to continue to invest in male privilege, or to make honorary men of academic women. If it is the case that, suddenly, men come to know the ways in which women might have to adjust to meet the current male standard, men might need to embark on mentoring programs. Could it be possible, for instance, that a new mentoring program arises from the ashes of the virus to teach men how to adequately reflect caring duties in grant submissions? How might men be otherwise mentored to achieve a female standard that, for instance, educates them on how to balance newly acquired hours spent in domestic work—with or without children—against the demands of their careers?

We do not know if such a notion will ever come to pass but, as both Krutikiva (Webber, 2020) and AbiRafeh (2020) both indicate, the possibility now exists. Policies that advance neoliberal ideals have long been justified—and opposition to them discredited—using Margaret Thatcher's famous line that "there is no alternative." This notion is reproduced in universities framing their responses to COVID-19 as a fait accompli—the inevitable result of unfortunate circumstances. Yet the neoliberal assumptions that underpin these responses illustrate that choices are being made and force us to ask whether the emergency we face necessitates this particular response.

Instead, we should see this as but one approach that is rooted in a vision of the university we do not need to support. Liminal times, in which the established social order is suspended, are opportunities, and this is an opportunity for university communities to have a broad discussion about gender relations in the university, what we think they should be like, and how to move toward that goal. Mentoring in all of its current forms cannot get us there. But perhaps an appreciation of the other can start us on the road.

We wanted to rehearse just one more idea on that front—a final provocation or at least something to think about. We've indicated throughout our book that mentors and mentees are cyclically involved in the creation of sameness, something we have suggested is responsible for the failure to shift the current state of play. When we think of this in connection with the university's advisement, made through the Global Institute for Women's Leadership, that it will take roughly a century for gender equity to be achieved under current conditions, we must contemplate the role of the past. We think in fact that a very important and specific reliance is made upon "the past." The past of gendered inequity is cleaved from the present—in which something is being done about that, by the university, which in its transparent remarks gets clear of the long shadow cast by the bad old days of accepting gender inequity. It will be, the Global Institute promises, a thing of the past. Right now, so the story goes, the university understands everything it needs to understand about gendered inequity to ensure intervention and rectification. But it is utterly critical to consider the terms in which gender inequity is consigned to the past: that is, in every way except the embodied. The past of gendered inequity and the declarations of its present demise constitute an important opposition that permits universities (and other entities) to operate conditions of pay and other inequities, but they might not be contemporarily experienced as oppositions by the bodies who live in such conditions. For them—for women like Kylie for instance—the past cannot be said to be over—indeed, it appears to stretch well into the future. There is a huge difference between declarations of compartmentalised time and the experience of the flesh—indeed, they are two different registers of temporal experience.

It's obvious from our offering that we dispute the notion that gender inequity is an historical hangover that is over, and that all we're really waiting for is for new institutional knowledge breakthroughs—such as those proffered by the Global Institute for Women's Leadership—to catch up. The relegation of inequity to the past and equity to the present forms a temporal complex in which gender inequity continues to thrive under conditions of the production and reproduction of sameness. Morris's (2008) concept of provisional time is instructive here.

Remarking on the insulin-dependent diabetic body, Morris (2008) speculates on how the experience of being answerable to an authority—here insulin—can impose a different registration of time for diabetic bodies than for non-insulin-dependent bodies. Morris begins by remarking that one of the key moments in the child-parent relationship is the moment that child becomes knowledgeable and experienced enough to take up the burden of caring that, hitherto, had been carried by her parents. Turning parental authority into responsibility and the care of the self, the child is no longer answerable to the parent. Ill physical or mental health, poverty, unemployment, and under- or absent education can effectively delay or halt that pivotal moment that Morris notes places a person into an ecstatic relationship of freedom with time. Insulin-dependent diabetes presents a barrier to that absolute freedom, for no diabetic could elect to abandon medical curfews—to do so could result in their death. The upshot for Morris is that diabetic medication effectively maintains a regimen of parental authority from which they could never be free.

Participation in the cycle of replication of success perhaps presents similar inhibitors to freedom—from institutional patriarchy. Female bodies remain trapped in a patriarchal time from which it cannot be free while the institution continues to produce sameness of our difference. The difference here is that while diabetics are treated a certain way to preserve their lives, women are made over into the image of senior women—and, actually, men. That reproduction of institutional patriarchy is made in bodies—not in historical time periods that are somehow catching up with us. That means, we think, that they're within our will to change. We shall see. Time—as we embody it—will tell.

Bibliography

AbiRafeh, L. 2020. Patriarchy and the pandemic: Rethinking "women's work" in a post-COVID world. https://www.mei.edu/publications/patriarchy-and-pandemic-rethinking-womens-work-post-covid-world.

Acker, J. 1990. Hierarchies, jobs, bodies: A theory of gendered organizations. *Gender and Society* 4 (2): 139–58.

Agrawal, A., and C. Gibson, eds. 2001. *Communities and the environment: Ethnicity, gender, and the state in community-based conservation.* New Brunswick, NJ: Rutgers University Press.

Ahmed, S. 2006. Doing diversity work in higher education in Australia. *Educational Philosophy and Theory* 38 (6): 745–68.

———. 2012. *On being included: Racism and diversity in institutional life.* Durham, NC: Duke University Press.

Anderson, E., and A. Shannon. 1988. Toward a conceptualization of mentoring. *Journal of Teacher Education* 39 (1): 38–42.

———. 1995. Toward a conceptualization of mentoring. In T. Kerry and A. S. Mayes (eds.), *Issues in mentoring* (pp. 25–34). London: Routledge.

Arendt, H. 1998. *The human condition.* Chicago: University of Chicago Press.

Art of Mentoring. 2020. https://www.artofmentoring.net/mentoring-programs-and-community.

Australian Human Rights Commission. 2017. *Change the course: National report on sexual assault and sexual harassment at Australian universities.* Sydney: Australian Human Rights Commission.

Australian National University (ANU). 2019a. *ANU awarded Bronze Athena SWAN accreditation.* www.anu.edu.au/news/all-news/anu-awarded-bronze-sage-athena-swan-accreditation.

———. 2019b. Gender equity & inclusion. www.anu.edu.au/about/strategic-planning/gender-equity-inclusion.

———. 2019c. Mentoring makes for an extended family. https://medicalschool.anu.edu.au/news-events/news/mentoring-makes-extended-family.

———. 2019d. The women behind Kambri's buildings. www.anu.edu.au/news/all-news/the-women-behind-kambri%E2%80%99s-buildings.

————. 2020. Mentor Walks celebrates 1 year in Canberra. www.anu.edu.au/news/all-news/mentor-walks-celebrates-1-year-in-canberra.

Australian Research Council. 2018. *Gender and the research workforce*. Report. https://dataportal.arc.gov.au/ERA/GenderWorkforceReport/2018.

Bacchi, C. 2000. The seesaw effect: Down goes affirmative action, up comes workplace diversity. *Journal of Interdisciplinary Gender Studies* 5 (2): 64–83.

Bagihole, B., and J. Goode. 2001. The contradiction of the myth of individual merit, and the reality of a patriarchal support system in academic careers—a feminist investigation. *European Journal of Women's Studies* 8 (2): 161–80.

Bagilhole, B., and K. White 2013. *Generation and Gender in Academia*. London: Palgrave Macmillan

Bailyn, L. 2003. Academic careers and gender equity: Lessons learned from MIT. *Gender, Work and Organization* 10 (2): 137–53.

Bansel, P., and B. Davies. 2010. Through a love of what neoliberalism puts at risk. In J. Blackmore, M. Brennan, and L. Zipin (eds.), *Re-positioning university governance and academic work* (pp. 133–45). Rotterdam: Sense.

Bell, E., K. Golombisky, G. Singh, and K. Hirschmann. 2000. To all the girls I've loved before: Academic love letters on mentoring, power, and desire. *Communication Theory* 10:27–48.

Bell, S. 2009. *Women in science: Maximising productivity, diversity and innovation*. Canberra: Federation of Australian Scientific and Technological Societies (FASTS).

Bell, S., and R. Bentley. 2005. *Women in research*. Discussion paper prepared for the Australian Vice Chancellors' Committee National Colloquium of Senior Women Executives, Griffith University, Brisbane.

Berlant, L. 2011. *Cruel optimism*. Durham, NC: Duke University Press.

Bhabha, H. 1994. *The location of culture*. London: Routledge.

Birchall, C. 2011. Introduction to "Secrecy and Transparency": The politics of opacity and openness. *Theory, Culture and Society* 28 (7/8): 7–25.

Black, A., and S. Garvis, eds. 2018. *Lived experiences of women in academia: Metaphors, manifestos and memoir*. Abingdon: Routledge.

Blackmore, J. 2014. "Wasting talent"? Gender and the problematics of academic disenchantment and disengagement with leadership. *Higher Education Research and Development* 33 (1): 86–99.

————. 2015. Disciplining academic women: Gender restructuring and the labour of research in entrepreneurial universities. In M. Thornton (ed.), *Through a glass darkly: The social sciences look at the neoliberal university* (pp. 179–94). Canberra: ANU Press.

Blackmore, J., and J. Sachs. 2007. *Performing and reforming leaders: Gender, educational restructuring, and organizational change*. Albany: State University of New York Press.

Boden, R., and D. Epstein. 2006. Managing the research imagination? *Globalisation Societies and Education* 4 (2): 223–36.

Bourdieu, P. 1988. *Homo academicus*. Stanford, CA: Stanford University Press.

————. 1990. *The logic of practice*. Cambridge: Polity.

The Bulletin. 2007, May 1. Heffernan targets "barren" Gillard. https://web.archive.o rg/web/20070505022032/http://bulletin.ninemsn.com.au/article.aspx?id=264308.

Burkinshaw, P. 2015. *Higher education, leadership and women vice chancellors: Fitting into communities of practice of masculinities.* Basingstoke, UK: Palgrave.

Bushardt, S., C. Fretwell, and B. Holdnak. 1991. The mentor/protege relationship: A biological perspective. *Human Relations* 44 (6): 619–39.

Campbell, K. 1998. The discursive performance of femininity: Hating Hillary. *Rhetoric and Public Affairs* 1 (1): 1–19.

Carmody, M. 2013. The neoliberal university in Australia: Permanent crisis. *Revista Congreso Universidad* 2 (3): 1–6.

Carruthers, J. 1993. The principles and practices of mentoring. In B. J. Caldwell and E. M. A. Carter (eds.), *The return of the mentor: Strategies for workplace learning* (pp. 9–24). London: Falmer.

Clark, T., S.W. Floyd, and M. Wright. 2006. On the review process and journal development, *Journal of Management Studies*, 43 (3): 655–664.

Clawson, J. 1980. Mentoring in managerial careers. In C. B. Derr (ed.), *Work, family and the career* (pp. 144–65). New York: Praeger.

Clouder, D., and A. Adefila. 2014. The "gift exchange": A metaphor for understanding the relationship between educator commitment and student effort on placement. *International Journal of Practice-Based Learning in Health and Social Care* 2 (2): 54–64.

Coates, L., and A. Wade. 2004. Telling it like it isn't: Obscuring perpetrator responsibility for violent crime. *Discourse and Society* 15 (5): 3–30.

Cockburn, C. 1991. *In the way of women: Men's resistance to sex equality in organizations.* New York: ILR Press.

Cohen, A. 1985. *The symbolic construction of community.* London: Tavistock.

Colley, H. 2003. *Mentoring for social inclusion: A critical approach to nurturing mentor relationships.* London: Routledge.

Cooper, S. 2007. Academic Darwinism: The (logical) end of the Dawkins era. *Arena Journal*, 28: 107–17.

Daloz, L. 1983. Mentors: Teachers who make a difference. *Change* 15 (6): 24–27.

Dalton, B. 2011. Assessing achievement relative to opportunity: Evaluating and rewarding academic performance fairly. Discussion paper. Equity and Diversity Centre. Melbourne: Monash University.

David, M. 2014. *Feminism, gender and universities: Politics passions and pedagogies.* Farnham, UK: Ashgate.

Davies, B., and P. Bansel. 2010. Governmentality and academic work: Shaping the hearts and minds of academic workers. *Journal of Curriculum Theorizing* 26 (3): 5–20.

Davis, G. 2012. The Australian idea of a university. *Meanjin* 72 (3): 32–48.

Deem, R., S. Hillyard, and M. Reed. 2008. *Knowledge, higher education, and the new managerialism: The changing management of UK universities.* Oxford: Oxford University Press.

Deem, R., and J. Ozga. 1997. Women managing for diversity in a post-modern world. In C. Marshall (ed.), *Feminist critical policy analysis: A perspective from post-secondary education* (pp. 25–40). London: Falmer.

Dennis, S. 2016. *Smokefree: A social, moral and political atmosphere.* London: Bloomsbury.

Derrida, J. (1967) 1978. *Writing and difference.* Chicago: University of Chicago Press.

———. 1992. *Given time: 1. Counterfeit money.* Chicago: University of Chicago Press.

Derrida, J., with M. Ferraris. 2001. A taste for the secret. G. Donis (trans.). In G. Donis and D. Webb (eds.), *A taste for the secret* (pp. 1–92). Cambridge, UK: Polity.

Devos, A. 2004. The project of self, the project of others: Mentoring, women and the fashioning of the academic subject. *Studies in Continuing Education* 26 (1): 67–80.

———. 2008. Where enterprise and equity meet: The rise of mentoring for women in Australian university. *Discourse: Studies in the cultural politics of education* 29 (2):195–200.

de Vries, J. 2011. Rethinking mentoring: Pursuing an organisational gender change agenda. In *Mentoring for change: A focus on mentors and their role in advancing gender equality* (pp. 12–26). Fribourg, Switzerland: eument-net.

Diamond, C. 2010. A memoir of co-mentoring: The "we" that is "me." *Mentoring and Tutoring: Partnership in Learning* 18 (2): 199–209.

Diprose, R. 2000. What is (feminist) philosophy? In "Going Australian: Reconfiguring Feminism and Philosophy." Special issue. *Hypatia* 15 (2): 115–32.

———. 2002. *Corporeal generosity: On giving with Nietzsche, Merleau-Ponty, and Levinas.* New York: State University of New York Press.

Dobbins, K., and P. Fell. 2019. Using the notion of "gift exchange" to explore effective mentoring relationships in the placement setting. *Teaching in Higher Education: Critical Perspectives* 25 (3): 334–49.

Donley, S., and C. Baird. 2017. The overtaking of undertaking: Gender beliefs in a feminizing occupation. *Sex Roles* 77 (1/2): 97–112.

Donovan, J. 1990. The concept and role of the mentor. In *Nurse Education Today* 10: 294–98.

Duffy, C. 2020, June 19. University fees to be overhauled, some course costs to double as domestic student places boosted. ABC News. www.abc.net.au/news/2020-06-19/university-fees-tertiary-education-overhaul-course-costs/12367742.

Ely, R., and D. Meyerson. 2000. Advancing gender equity in organizations: The challenge and importance of maintaining a gender narrative. *Organization* 7 (4): 589–608.

Ehrlich, S. 2001. *Representing rape: Language and sexual consent.* London: Routledge.

Epstein, D., R. Boden, R. Deem, F. Rizvi, and S. Wright, eds. 2008. *World yearbook of education 2008: Geographies of knowledge, geometries of power—Framing the future of higher education.* Abingdon Oxon: Routledge.

Evans, G. 2019, Feb. 15. 2019 State of the university: Chancellor's speech. Australian National University. www.anu.edu.au/news/all-news/2019-state-of-the-university-chancellors-speech.

Ferrara, E. 2020, June 29. Baby matters: Gender politics beyond COVID-19 and the "aunts" of academia. *Academic Matters*. https://academicmatters.ca/baby-matters-gender-politics-in-academia-beyond-covid-19.

Ferree, M., and K. Zippel. 2015. Gender equality in the age of academic capitalism: Cassandra and Pollyanna interpret university restructuring. *Social Politics* 22 (4): 561–84.

Feteris, S. 2012. *The role of women academics in Australian universities*. Proceedings of the 20th Australian Institute of Physics Congress, Sydney.

Field, B., and T. Field, eds. 1994. *Teachers as mentors: A practical guide*. London: Falmer.

Finley, M. 1982. *The world of Odysseus*. New York: New York Review Books.

Fitzgerald, T. 2014. *Women leaders in higher education: Shattering myths*. New York: Routledge.

Fitzgerald, T., and J. Wilkinson. 2010. *Travelling towards a mirage? Gender, leadership and higher education*. Mt. Gravatt: Post Pressed.

Forsyth, H. 2014. *A history of the modern Australian university*. Sydney: NewSouth Publishing.

Fotaki, M. 2013. No woman is like a man (in academia): The masculine symbolic order and the unwanted female body. *Organization Studies* 34 (9): 1251–75.

Freeman, J. 2011. *Argument structure: Representation and theory*. New York: Springer.

Gale, F. 1998. Who nurtures the nurturers? Senior women in universities. In D. Cohen, A. Lee, J. Newman, A. Payne, H. Scheeres, L. Shoemark, and S. Tiffin (eds.), *Winds of change: Women and the culture of universities* (pp. 290–95). Sydney: University of Technology.

Gannon, S., K. Giedre, J. McLean, M. Perrier, E. Swan, I. Vanni, and H. van Rijswijk. 2015. Uneven relationalities, collective biography, and sisterly affect in neoliberal universities. *Feminist Formations* 27 (3): 189–216.

Gardiner, M., M. Tiggemann, H. Kearns, and K. Marshall. 2007. Show me the money!: An empirical analysis of mentoring outcomes for women in academia. *Higher Education Research and Development* 26 (4): 425–42.

Gatens, M. 1996. *Imaginary bodies: Ethics, power and corporeality*. London: Routledge.

Gaviola, A. 2020. Prolonged recession ahead if there isn't a childcare solution. *Economist*. BNN Bloomberg News Service. www.bnnbloomberg.ca/prolonged-recession-ahead-if-there-isn-t-a-childcare-solution-economist-1.1466063.

Giddens, A. 1981. *Agency, institution, and time-space analysis. Advances in social theory and methodology*. Boston: Routledge and Kegan Paul.

Gill, R. 2010. Breaking the silence: Hidden injuries of the neoliberal university. In R. Ryan-Flood and R. Gill (eds.), *Secrecy and silence in the research process: Feminist reflections* (pp. 228–244). Oxon: Routledge.

Gluckman, M. 1958. *Analysis of a social situation in modern Zululand*. Manchester: Manchester University Press.

Graeber, D. 2000. Give it away. *In These Times* 24 (19). https://inthesetimes.com/iss ue/24/19/graeber2419.html.

———. 2014. On the moral grounds of economic relations: A Maussian approach. *Journal of Classical Sociology* 14 (1): 65–77.

Gregory, C. A. 1997. *Savage money: The anthropology and politics of commodity exchange*. Amsterdam: Harwood Academic.

Grimshaw, P., and R. Francis. 2014. Academic women and research leadership in twentieth-century Australia. In J. Damousi, K. Rubenstein, and M. Tomsic (eds.), *Diversity in leadership: Australian women, past and present* (pp. 207–37). Canberra: ANU Press.

Grummell, B., D. Devine, and K. Lynch. 2009. The care-less manager: Gender, care and new managerialism in higher education. *Gender and Education* 21 (2): 191–208.

Gulam, W., and M. Zulfiqar. 1998. Mentoring—Dr. Plum's elixir and the alchemist's stone. *Mentoring and Tutoring* 5 (3): 46–56.

Gunn, J. 2010. On speech and public release. *Rhetoric and Public Affairs* 13 (2): 1–41.

Habermas, J. 1989. *The structural transformation of the public sphere: An inquiry into a category of bourgeois society*. Trans. T. Burger and F. Lawrence. Cambridge: Polity.

Hacker, D. 2018. Crying on campus. In Y. Taylor and K. Lahad (eds.), *Feeling academic in the neoliberal university: Feminist flights, fights and failures* (pp. 281–99). London: Palgrave Macmillan.

Harding, N., J. Ford, and M. Fotaki. 2013. Is the "f"-word still dirty?: A past, present and future of/for feminist and gender studies in organization. *Organization* 20 (1): 51–65.

Harvey, D. 2005. *A brief history of neoliberalism*. Oxford: Oxford University Press.

Harvey, L., and J. Newton. 2004. Transforming quality evaluation. *Quality in Higher Education* 10 (2): 149–65.

Hey, V., and S. Bradford. 2004. The return of the repressed? The gender politics of emergent forms of professionalism in education. *Journal of Education Policy* 19 (6): 691–713.

Hiatt, L. 1982. Traditional attitudes to land resources. In R. M. Berndt (ed.), *Aboriginal sites, rites and resource development* (pp. 13–26). Perth: University of Western Australia Press.

Ingold, T. 2000. Building, dwelling, living: How animals and people make themselves at home in the world. In T. Ingold (ed.), *The perception of the environment: Essays on livelihood, dwelling and skill* (pp. 172–88). London: Routledge.

———. 2007. *Lines: A brief history*. London: Routledge.

———. 2011. *Redrawing anthropology: Materials, movements, lines*. Farnham: Ashgate.

Jackson, M. 2002. *The politics of storytelling: Violence, transgression, and intersubjectivity*. Copenhagen: Museum Tusculanum Press.

Jarvis, P. 1995. Towards a philosophical understanding of mentoring. *Nurse Education Today* 15: 414–19.

Jaspers, K. (1949) 2011. *The origin and goal of history.* New York: Routledge.

Jayasuriya, K. 2021 COVID-19, markets and the crisis of the higher education regulatory state: The case of Australia, *Globalizations*, 18 (4): 584–599.

Jenkins, F. 2014. Singing the post-discrimination blues: Notes for a critique of academic meritocracy. In K. Hutchinson and F. Jenkins (eds.), *Women in philosophy: What needs to change?* (pp. 81–102). New York: Oxford University Press.

Johnson, D. 2013. *What we owe to each other: An interview with David Graeber.* https://bostonreview.net/archives/BR37.1/david_graeber_debt_economics_occupy_wall_street.php.

Johnson, H. 2016. *Pipelines, pathways, and institutional leadership: An update on the status of women in higher education.* Washington, DC: American Council on Education.

Jones, S. 2013. The "star" academics are so often white and male. *The Guardian*, April 23. www.theguardian.com/education/2013/apr/22/university-jobs-not-beingadvertised.

Kalbfleisch, P., and J. Keyton. 1995. Power and equality in mentoring relationships. In P. Kalbfleisch and M. Cody (eds.), *Gender, power, and communication in human relationships* (pp. 189–212). Hillsdale, NJ: Lawrence Erlbaum Associates.

Kamvounias, P., S. McGrath-Champ, and J. Yip. 2008. "Gifts" in mentoring: Mentees' reflections on an academic development program. *International Journal for Academic Development* 13 (1): 17–25.

Kapferer, B. 2003. Introduction: Outside all reason—Magic, sorcery and epistemology in anthropology. In B. Kapferer (ed.), *Beyond rationalism: Rethinking magic, witchcraft and sorcery* (pp. 1–30). New York: Berghahn.

Katz, Jack. 1999. *How emotions work.* Chicago: University of Chicago Press.

Katz, Jackson. 2017, Oct. 18. We talk about women being raped, not men raping women. www.jacksonkatz.com/news/talk-women-raped-not-men-raping-women.

Klein, E. 1967. *A comprehensive etymological dictionary of the English language: Dealing with the origin of words and their sense development thus illustrating the history of civilisation and culture.* Vol. 2. Amsterdam: Elsevier.

Klocker, N., and D. Drozdzewski. 2012. Commentary: Career progress relative to opportunity: How many papers is a baby "worth"? *Environment and Planning A* 44 (6): 1271–77.

Kreamer, A. 2011. *It's always personal: Navigating emotion in the new workplace.* New York: Random House.

Lafferty, G., and J. Fleming. 2000. The restructuring of academic work in Australia: Power, management and gender. *British Journal of Sociology Education* 21 (2): 257–67.

Larkins, F. 2018. *Male students remain underrepresented in Australian universities. Should we be concerned?*://melbourne-cshe.unimelb.edu.au/lh-martin-institute/insights/gender-enrollment-trends-flarkins.

Lerner, S. 2020. A hack for the modern mentor. https://suzannelerner.com/sl-blog/a-hack-for-the-modern-mentor-mix-one-part-generosity-with-one-part-selfishness-for-lifelong-rewards.

Lindell, J. 2017, March 17. ANU and the gods face legal battle. www.woroni.com.au/news/anu-and-the-gods-face-legal-battle.

Lipton, B. 2015. A new "ERA" of women and leadership: The gendered impact of quality assurance in Australian higher education. *Australian Universities' Review* 57 (2): 60–70.

———. 2020. *Academic women in neoliberal times*. Cham, Switzerland: Springer.

Little, J. W. 1990. The mentor phenomenon and the social organization of teaching. *Review of Research in Education* 16 (1): 297–351.

Lorenz, C. 2012. "If you're so smart, why are you under surveillance?" Universities, neoliberalism, and new public management. *Critical Inquiry* 38 (3): 599–629.

MacFarlane, B. 2018. Women professors, pay, promotion and academic housekeeping. Wonkhe (blog) https://wonkhe.com/blogs/women-professors-pay-promotion-and-academic-housekeeping/.

Manne, K. 2017. *Down girl: The logic of misogyny*. Ithaca, NY: Oxford University Press.

Marginson, S., and M. Considine. 2000. *The enterprise university: Power, governance and reinvention in Australia*. Cambridge: Cambridge University Press.

Massey, D. 1994. *Space, place and gender*. Cambridge: Polity.

Mauss, M. 1925. *The gift: The form and reason for exchange in archaic societies*. London: Routledge.

May, R., D. Peetz, and G. Strachan. 2013. The casual academic workforce and labour market segmentation in Australia. *Labour & Industry* 23 (3): 258–75.

Megginson, D., and D. Clutterbuck, eds. 1995. *Mentoring in action: A practical guide for managers*. London: Kogan Page.

Menzies, H., and J. Newson. 2008. Time, stress and intellectual engagement in academic work: Exploring gender difference. *Gender, Work and Organization* 15 (5): 504–22.

Merriam, S. 1983. Mentors and protégés: A critical review of the literature. *Adult Education Quarterly* 33 (3): 161–73.

Meschitti, V., and H. Lawton-Smith. 2017. Does mentoring make a difference for women academics? Evidence from the literature and a guide for future research. *Journal of Research in Gender Studies* 7 (1): 166–99.

Miller, D. 2005. *Materiality*. Durham, NC: Duke University Press.

Monaghan, J., and N. Lunt. 1992. Mentoring: Persons, processes, practice and problems. *British Journal of Educational Studies* 40 (3): 117–33.

Moodley, K., and A. Gouws. 2020, August 7. How women in academia are feeling the brunt of COVID-19. *The Conversation*. https://theconversation.com/how-women-in-academia-are-feeling-the-brunt-of-covid-19-144087.

Morley, L. 1999. *Organising feminisms: The micropolitics of the academy*. Basingstoke: Palgrave Macmillan.

———. 2003. Gendered universities in globalized economies: Power, careers and sacrifices. *McGill Journal of Education* 38 (3): 494–95. http://mje.mcgill.ca/article/view/8713/6656.

———. 2011. Misogyny posing as measurement: Disrupting the feminisation crisis discourse. *Contemporary Social Science* 6 (2): 223–35.

————. 2013. The rules of the game: Women and the leaderist turn in higher education. *Gender and Education* 25 (1): 116–31.

Mullen, C., and J. Hutinger. 2008. At the tipping point? The role of formal faculty mentoring in changing university research cultures. *Professional Development in Education* 34 (2): 181–204.

Murray, M. 1991. *Beyond the myths and magic of mentoring*. San Francisco: Jossey Bass.

Newman, J. 2013. Spaces of power: Feminism, neoliberalism and gendered labor. *Social Politics* 20 (2): 200–221.

Ng, L. 2020. Where have all the surpluses gone? https://overland.org.au/2020/09/where-have-all-the-surpluses-gone/.

Noble, G., and S. Poynting. 2010. White lines: The intercultural politics of everyday movement in social spaces. *Journal of Intercultural Studies* 31 (5): 489–505.

Ortner, S. 1974. Is female to male as nature is to culture? In M. Z. Rosaldo and L. Lamphere (eds.), *Woman, Culture, and Society* (pp. 67–87). Stanford, CA: Stanford University Press.

Orwell. G. 1946. *Politics and the English language*. London: Horizon.

Parsloe, E. 1995. *Coaching, mentoring and assessing: A practical guide to developing competence*. London: Kogan Page.

PeopleGrove. 2020. www.peoplegrove.com.

Petersen, E. 2009. Resistance and enrollment in the enterprise university: An ethno-drama in three acts, with appended reading. *Journal of Education Policy* 24 (4): 409–22.

Peterson, N. 1993. Demand sharing: Reciprocity and the pressure for generosity among foragers. *American Anthropologist* 95 (4): 860–74.

Pfund, C., A. Byars-Winston, J. Branchaw, J. Hurtado, and K. Eagan. 2016. Defining attributes and metrics of effective research mentoring relationships. *AIDS and Behavior* 20 (2): 238–48.

Phillips, K. 2013, July 2. Australia's universities: From elite institutions to degree factories? *Rear Vision*, ABC Radio National. www.abc.net.au/radionational/programs/rearvision/4792034.

Phillips, M. 2014. Re-writing corporate environmentalism: Ecofeminism, corporeality and the language of feeling. *Gender, Work and Organization* 21 (5): 443–58.

Pillay, S., R. Kluvers, S. Abhayawansa, and V. Vedran. 2013. An exploratory study into work/family balance within the Australian higher education sector. *Higher Education Research and Development* 32 (2): 228–43.

Pitt-Rivers, J. 1977. *The fate of shechem or the politics of sex: Essays in the anthropology of the Mediterranean* (pp. 94–112). Cambridge: Cambridge University Press.

Probert, B. 2005. "I just couldn't fit it in": Gender and unequal outcomes in academic careers. *Gender, Work and Organization* 12 (1): 50–72.

Puwar, N. 2004. *Space invaders: Race, gender and bodies out of place*. Oxford: Berg.

Quinlan, K. 1999. Enhancing mentoring and networking of junior academic women: What, why, and how? *Journal of Higher Education Policy and Management* 21 (1): 31–42.

Rafferty, L., B. Dalton, B. Hill, I. Saris, L. Atkinson-Barrett, and L. Maynard. 2010. *Consideration of merit relative to opportunity in employment-related decisions.* Discussion paper presented to Group of Eight HR Directors Staff Equity Subcommittee Project.

Randell-Moon, H., S. Saltmarsh, and W. Sutherland-Smith. 2013. The living dead and the dead living: Contagion and complicity in contemporary universities. In A. Whelan, R. Walker, and C. Moore (eds.), *Zombies in the academy: Living death in higher education* (pp. 53–65). Bristol: Intellect.

Rapport, N. 2003. *I am dynamite: An alternative anthropology of power.* New York: Psychology Press.

Reay, M. (F. Merlan, ed.) 2014. *Wives and wanderers in a New Guinea highlands society.* Canberra: ANU Press.

Richards, T. 1993. *The imperial archive: Knowledge and the fantasy of empire.* London: Verso.

Riddell, J. 2016. Examining teaching and learning through a neoliberal lens: On faith, metrics and the neoliberal university. www.universityaffairs.ca/opinion/ adventures-in-academe/teaching-learning-neoliberal-lens.

Rieu, E. V., trans. 1946. *The Odyssey.* New York: Penguin.

Roberts, A. 1999. Homer's Mentor: The origins of the term mentor. *History of Education Society Bulletin* 64 (1): 313–329.

Roberts, L. 2018. Indigenous elders unite to name new ANU precinct "Kambri." Riotact. https://www.the-riotact.com/ indigenous-elders-unite-to-name-new-anu-precinct-kambri/231565.

Roche, G. 1979. Much ado about mentoring. *Harvard Business Review* 57 (1): 14–20.

Rosser, S., S. Barnard, M. Carnes, F. Munir. 2019. Athena SWAN and ADVANCE: Effectiveness and lessons learned. *The Lancet* 393 (10171): 604–8.

Rowbotham, J. 2020. ANU to be Oxbridge of the South. *The Australian*, Feb. 11.

Sahlins, M. 1972. *Stone Age economics.* Chicago: Aldine.

Savigny, H. 2014. Women, know your limits: Cultural sexism in academia. *Gender and Education* 26 (7): 794–809.

Schmidt, .B. 2021. The 7:30 Report. May 20 2021, ABC Television. https://iview.ab c.net.au/video/NC2101H080S00).

Schmitt, M. 2010, Feb. 15. Transparency for what? *The American Prospect.* https:// prospect.org/special-report/transparency-what.

Shea, G. 1992. *Mentoring: A guide to the basics.* London: Kogan Page.

Shore, C., and L. McLauchlan. 2012. "Third mission" activities, commercialisation and academic entrepreneurs. *Social Anthropology* 20 (3): 267–86.

Skeggs, B. 2014. Values beyond value? Is anything beyond the logic of capital? *British Journal of Sociology* 65 (1): 1–20.

Slaughter, S., and L. Leslie. 1997. *Academic capitalism: Politics, policies, and the entrepreneurial university.* Baltimore: Johns Hopkins University Press.

Smith, K., F. Else, and P. Crookes. 2014. Engagement and academic promotion: A review of the literature. *Higher Education Research and Development* 33 (4): 836–47.

Smith, R., and G. Alred. 1993. The impersonation of wisdom. In D. McIntyre, H. Hagger, and M. Wilkin (eds.), *Mentoring: Perspectives on school-based teacher education* (pp. 103–16). London: Kogan Page.

Smyth, J. 2017. *The toxic university: Zombie leadership, academic rock stars and neoliberal ideology.* London: Palgrave.

Spencer, M. 2019. Designing equality on campus. https://etcetera.org.au/power/designing-equality-on-campus.

Stammers, P. 1992. The Greeks had a word for it (five millennia of mentoring). *British Journal of In-Service Education* 18 (2): 76–80.

Steiner, P. 2003. Gifts of blood and organs: The market and "fictitious" commodities. *Revue française de sociologie* 5 (44): 147–62.

Strachan, G., D. Peetz, G. Whitehouse, J. Bailey, K. Broadbent, R. May, C. Troup, and M. Nesic. 2016. *Women, careers and universities: Where to from here?* Brisbane: Centre for Work, Organisation and Wellbeing, Griffith University.

Thornton, M. 2013. The mirage of merit: Reconstituting the "ideal academic." *Australian Feminist Studies* 28 (76): 127–43.

———, ed. 2015. *Through a glass darkly: The social sciences look at the neoliberal university.* Canberra: ANU Press.

Tickle, L. 1993. The wish of Odysseus? In D. McIntyre, H. Hagger, and M. Wilkin (eds.), *Mentoring: Perspectives on school-based teacher education* (pp. 190–205). London: Kogan Page.

Times Higher Education. 2019. Impact rankings 2019 by SDG: Gender equality. www.timeshighereducation.com/rankings/impact/2019/gender-equality#!/page/0/length/25/sort_by/rank/sort_order/asc/cols/undefined.

Titmuss, R. 1970. *The gift relationship: From human blood to social policy.* London: School of Economics Books.

Tommasini, S., P. Nasser, and K. Jepsen. 2007. Sexual dimorphism affects tibia size and shape but not tissue-level mechanical properties. *Bone* 40:498–505.

Tudge, A. 2021. The 7:30 Report. May 20 2021, ABC Television. https://iview.abc.net.au/video/NC2101H080S00).

Turner, V. 1967. *The forest of symbols.* Ithaca, NY: Cornell University Press.

Tzanakou, C., and R. Pearce. 2018. Moderate feminism within or against the neoliberal university? The example of Athena SWAN. *Gender Work and Organization* 26 (8): 1191–1211.

Urciuoli, B. 2010. Neoliberal education: preparing the student for the new workplace. In C. Greenhouse (ed.), *Ethnographies of neoliberalism* (pp. 162–176). Philadelphia: University of Pennsylvania Press.

van den Brink, M., and Y. Benschop. 2014. Gender in academic networking: The role of gatekeepers in professorial recruitment. *Journal of Management Studies* 51 (3): 460–92.

van der Weijden, I., R. Belder, P. van Arensbergen, and P. van den Besselaar. 2014. How do young tenured professors benefit from a mentor? Effects on management, motivation and performance. *Higher Education* 69 (1): 275–87.

Van Gennep, A. 1960. *The rites of passage.* London: Routledge and Kegan Paul.

Vira, B., and R. Jeffrey, eds. 2001. Introduction: Analytical issues in participatory natural resource management. In B. Vira and R. Jeffery (eds.), *Analytical issues in participatory natural resources* (pp. 1–16). Basingstoke, UK: Palgrave Macmillan.

Vu, C., and J. Doughney. 2007. Unequal outcomes for women academics in Australian universities: Reflections on Belinda Probert's "I just couldn't fit in." *Journal of Business Systems, Governance and Ethics* 2 (4): 55–65.

Watts, M. 2000. Contested communities, malignant markets, and gilded governance: Justice, resource extraction, and conservation in the tropics. In Charles Zerner (ed.), *People, plants, and justice: The politics of nature conservation* (pp. 21–51). New York: Columbia University Press.

Webb, C., and P. Shakespeare. 2008. Mentoring relationships in nurse education. *Nurse Education Today* 28 (5): 563–71.

Webber, A. 2020. Lockdown pressures on mothers could stall gender pay gap progress. *Personnel Today*. www.personneltoday.com/hr/lockdown-working-parents-ifs-report.

White, K., T. Carvalho, and S. Riordan. 2011. Gender, power and managerialism in universities. *Journal of Higher Education Policy and Management* 33 (2): 179–88.

Wilkinson, C. 2019. What role can Athena SWAN play in gender equality and science communication? *Journal of Science Communication* 18 (4): 1–7. doi. org/10.22323/2.18040306.

Williams, R. 1976. *Keywords*. London: Fontana.

Wilson, J., and N. Elman. 1990. Organizational benefits of mentoring. *The Executive* 4 (4): 88–94.

Winchester, H., and L. Browning. 2015. Gender equality in academia: A critical reflection. *Journal of Higher Education Policy and Management* 37 (3): 269–81.

Winchester, H., C. Chesterman, S. Lorenzo, and L. Browning. 2005. *The great barrier myth: An investigation of promotions policy and practice in Australian universities.* Canberra: Australian Vice-Chancellors' Committee.

Woroni, 2013, Oct. 30. *The ANU: Australia's Harvard?* www.woroni.com.au/news/the-anu-australias-harvard.

Index

AbiRafeh, Lina, 142–43
Aboriginal people, 127–28
accounting. *See* corporeal accounting
ACE. *See* American Council on Education
Les Adventures de Telemaque (Fenenlo), 37
Ahmed, S., 64
AHSSBL. *See* arts, humanities, social sciences, business and law
alterity, 131–34
American Council on Education (ACE): Moving the Needle initiative of, 29–30; Pipelines, Pathways, and Institutional Leadership report of, 28–29
Andrea (informant), 104–5
Annabel (informant), 68
ANU. *See* Australian National University
Arab region, 142–43
Arendt, Hannah, 88
Art of Mentoring (mentoring firm), 31
arts, humanities, social sciences, business and law (AHSSBL), 103
Athena (goddess), 23n2; buildings and, 87; Mentor role of, 20, 36–37; orientation of, 47–51; as perfection, 25; rebellion and, 101

Athena SWAN charter: accreditation levels, 103–4; AHSSBL added to, 103; ANU and, 102–4; awards of, 102–3; establishment of, 101; mandate of, 101–2; NIHR and, 103, 112n4; women unpaid and overworked in, 104–5
attractive, 16
Australian National University (ANU), 6; Athena SWAN and, 102–4; authorship orientation at, 16; in Canberra, 49, 80n1; challenges of, 49–51; community and, 31–32; COVID-19 impacting, 49–50; disobedience and, 18; equity and diversity at, 102; female oppression recognised at, 84; gender equity news page of, 106; GIWL and, 106; goodness of mentoring and, 33; honorary women and, 93–101; imitation by, 48–50; invitation only model for mentoring, 126–27; marketing of, 80n1; Naming Policy of, 96–97; as research institution, 52–53; study related to, 19; teaching versus research at, 99. *See also* Kambri precinct
authorship, orientation to, 15–17

About the Authors

Simone Dennis is a social anthropologist who received her PhD from the University of Adelaide in 2002. Simone's varied and wide-ranging anthropological interests (including in smoking and the politics of the air, citizenship and asylum seeking on Christmas Island, cultural traditions within scientific laboratories, affect in police work, and everyday alcohol use) coalesce around phenomenologically informed anthropological theories of embodiment, the senses, and power. Her work attends closely to the experiences of bodies as they encounter power, especially as it is brought to bear in the form of government policy; Simone pays particular attention to the smallest and least foregrounded of those encounters to search for and understand powerful micropolitics, including, for instance, in respiration and in swallowing. Her innovative scholarship on tobacco, conducted outside the dominant public health frame in which tobacco use is more usually studied, is the best-known substantial contribution to her standing as a thinker beyond the paradigm. Simone presently serves as associate dean for research engagement, impact and innovation in the College of Arts and Social Sciences at the Australian National University, and priorly served as head of the School of Archaeology and Anthropology.

Alison Behie completed her PhD in anthropology at the University of Calgary in 2010 where her dissertation research documented the long-term impact of a hurricane on the stress, nutrition and disease of a wild howler monkey population. In 2011, Alison was appointed as a lecturer in biological anthropology at the Australian National University. In her time at ANU, she has been promoted to associate professor and was both head of biological anthropology (2015–2020) and deputy head of school (2019–2021). She is currently the head of the School of Archaeology and Anthropology.

Her research interests focus on understanding the impact of environmental change on primates. She has spent two decades studying how wild primate populations respond to habitat change due to natural and anthropogenic causes. She was previously an Australian Research Council DECRA fellow where her research explored how the behaviour, reproduction and distribution of lemurs in Madagascar are impacted by frequent exposure to cyclones. She has extended this work on nonhuman primates to include humans by studying how natural disasters and stress impact birth outcomes and development in pregnant women.

Alison is also committed to advocating for women in academia, speaking on podcasts and at events about work-life balance and the struggles of juggling motherhood with having an academic job.

www.ingramcontent.com/pod-product-compliance
Lightning Source LLC
Chambersburg PA
CBHW022319280326
41932CB00010B/1162